PRIMARY SCHOOL GYMNASTICS

D0084335

PRIMARY SCHOOL GYMNASTICS

Teaching Movement Skills Successfully

Lawry Price

David Fulton Publishers

London

David Fulton Publishers Ltd
The Chiswick Centre, 414 Chiswick High Road, London W4 5TF

www.fultonpublishers.co.uk

David Fulton Publishers is a division of Granada Learning Limited,
part of the Granada Media group.

First published 2003
10 9 8 7 6 5 4 3 2 1

Copyright © 2003 Lawry Price

British Library Cataloguing in Publication Data
A catalogue record for this book is available from the British Library.

ISBN 1 85346 951 3

All rights reserved. No part of this publication may be reproduced, stored in a
retrieval system or transmitted, in any form or by any means, electronic,
mechanical, photocopying, or otherwise, without the prior permission of the
publishers.

GV
464.5
P75
2003

Typeset by Keyset Composition, Colchester, Essex
Printed and bound in Great Britain by Ashford Colour Press, Gosport, Hants

OLSON LIBRARY
NORTHERN MICHIGAN UNIVERSITY
MARQUETTE, MI 49855

Contents

Acknowledgements   vii

Introduction   ix

1   Using These Teaching Materials   1

2   A Rationale for Primary School Gymnastics   3

3   Motor Development   5

4   Ensuring Continuity and Progression in the Work   7

5   National Curriculum Physical Education   10

6   Developing the Work   13

7   A Checklist for Health and Safety in Gymnastic Activities   21

8   Gymnastics Teaching Material for Reception, Year 1 and Year 2   23

9   Gymnastics Teaching Material for Years 3 and 4   48

10   Gymnastics Teaching Material for Years 5 and 6   73

11   Further Gymnastic Themes   102

Appendix 1   Record Sheets for Assessment of Pupil Progress   107

Appendix 2   The Content of Primary Gymnastic Activity: Movement Vocabulary   109

Resources   111

Index   115

Acknowledgements

The teaching materials presented here are a personal contribution to effective teaching and learning in gymnastic activities for the primary school. In producing these I wish to express my sincere thanks to a number of different people for helping me to put these teaching materials together.

First, thanks go to all those teachers who have inspired me to think and adapt my own personal practice, and who have offered support and help in my teaching of gymnastics over the years. These include early mentors, fellow physical educationists and current practitioners who strive to provide the best possible experience for their charges through well planned, effectively delivered and enjoyable (and therefore worthwhile) activity. As one, they have appreciated the importance of this area of the curriculum as fundamental to learning in PE and the resultant benefits that children gain in acquiring greater motor competence. Particular thanks go to the teachers and children of Dundonald Primary School in Merton, who worked hard to add the photographic element to these materials.

Colleagues whose own teaching materials have provided reference points include authors in the field as well as a gallery of teaching colleagues who have willingly shared their practice and ideas for teaching gymnastics. I am heartened by the most recent publications in the field, particularly those that have plugged some gaps for early years' provision and prompted a more structured approach to PE for children in these important formative years.

My thanks are also extended to David Fulton Publishers for presenting the opportunity to publish these materials, and particularly to Helen Fairlie, who has supported me and displayed great patience throughout the project.

Finally, thanks go to the children I have taught (including my own!), who are the real inspiration and motivation behind the production of what I believe to be teaching materials that can support, guide, enthuse and convince fellow teachers that here is the essence and key to learning in PE in the primary school setting. I firmly believe that if gymnastic activities are taught well then the benefits to other areas of the PE curriculum will naturally follow. If a sense of challenge, adventure, fun and enjoyment is prompted at the same time, then what should result are worthwhile and meaningful outcomes for all involved in the process, teachers and children alike.

Introduction

I first qualified as a teacher in 1977 (a year in a period when teaching vacancies were not numerous) and deemed myself fortunate to secure a teaching post in a London LEA five-form entry 9–13 middle school. I was appointed as 'teacher responsible for PE and boys' games' and one of the biggest challenges in my fledgling career was to provide a meaningful gymnastics curriculum across the school. My own training had included a great deal of movement input, including ample opportunity to try out the ideas and teaching strategies through teaching practices at a range of schools (primary and secondary). Faced with the reality of planning, teaching and assessing gymnastics across four year groups, and convinced as I was that the activity area was the cornerstone of the PE curriculum, I set about confronting the challenge.

A starting point and reference base was necessary. I turned to a particularly reliable resource that I had discovered during my training, Don Buckland's book *Gymnastics: Activity in the Primary School* (1969). Here was what I needed to establish principles, organising strategies and features that I could adapt to my own teaching. I realised that it was crucial to develop and progress the gymnastic learning activities to cater for the 9–13 age range. Reference to Don's book, among others, stood me in good stead for many years and helped to serve a multitude of children's physical movement needs during that time.

There have been many additions to the world of books and resources to support teachers in their gymnastics teaching since the 1970s. The implementation of the National Curriculum for Physical Education in 1992 spawned a most welcome new supply of such materials. Since then, further revisions to the National Curriculum have seen a similar response from a range of professionals in the field. What is significant is that the non-statutory guidelines produced for the National Curriculum for PE in 1992 promoted a list of 'key gymnastic themes', which are all evidenced in Buckland's work and are presented here, in modified form.

Now engaged in initial teacher education, I have been motivated through the producion of these materials to promote what I feel remains the essence of PE activity within the primary school setting. I am utterly convinced that the basic skill competencies that children need to master are encapsulated within a well designed, continuous, progressive gymnastics curriculum. The control, coordination and discipline learnt from gymnastic activity provide the basis from which all other areas of movement draw, including such important elements to daily life as locomotion, general stability and manipulative skills.

What I have attempted to do here is to help teachers to develop their own knowledge base by providing a structure to their gymnastics teaching. I have adapted my teaching experience, reading and research to today's agenda, and hope that this material will provide others with the inspiration I received from earlier materials. They are carefully laid out so that there is a progressive feel to the work suggested here, with the potential to drop in to particular themes. It is intended that this book will be particularly useful to newly qualified teachers, but also provide supplementary ideas for the more experienced who need additional activity material.

I have designed the material presented here so that teachers may use it for reference, read it in order to plan the gymnastics curriculum and/or in order to stimulate sharing and debate amongst colleagues. By adopting such an approach primary teachers will all help to keep the teaching of gymnastic activities alive.

I believe the following guidelines are essential for successful practice supporting gymnastics teaching in our primary schools:

- plan units of work, themes and individual lesson activities thoroughly;
- expect children to be enthusiastic and receptive to gymnastic content and have high expectations of their achievements;
- be prepared to repeat and consolidate previous work in a variety of different ways and through different teaching approaches;
- set different or alternative tasks in floorwork and when the work moves on to apparatus;
- keep the work active and participatory with minimised instruction;
- create a positive learning environment by adopting and implementing good working routines, which need to be taught, learnt and applied – they don't just happen;
- continuously assess performance to inform on-going planning.

Finally, only through practice and accrued experience does one's own teaching improve. This takes time, but can only happen if we confront the challenge that gymnastics teaching presents us with. We owe children their right to move with increasing confidence, skills, control and precision.

1 Using These Teaching Materials

Drawing on my own teaching experience, as well as that of teachers whom I have worked alongside over the years, has brought home the key message that teaching gymnastics to primary school aged children presents a unique set of challenges. These often focus on ideas for practice, progression in the work and how to transfer the work covered on the floor (and therefore low-level apparatus) on to the more demanding large apparatus work. Supporting teachers' own development as effective practitioners in the area, as well as meeting their desire to provide meaningful and real learning opportunities for their children, has prompted this teaching resource. The teaching materials presented here aim to meet such needs, are prompts for ongoing work in the area and ultimately satisfy the remit of a gymnastics curriculum for primary aged children.

When help and support are called for in the teaching of primary school gymnastics it helps greatly if there is a basic framework in place in which to set potential work. Knowing what actions and movements to expect from children is a starting point, but an awareness of the dynamics involved is equally important if the work is to progress sequentially and in line with the growing bodies that primary children present us to work with. Picking out a number of progressive themes that cover key essentials can ensure the relevance and appropriateness of activity offered.

This book presents a thematic approach to learning through gymnastic activities. This is not 'new' but is a restatement that the aim of gymnastics provision in our primary schools is to teach movement by focusing clearly on the body, its constituent parts and how these work together with the natural actions that young children perform daily in their everyday movement, play and recreation. The starting point is to build on what children do quite naturally in their everyday lives, through their play and their natural inclination to move through their immediate environment.

The materials are divided for ease of reference into three key age phases:

- Reception, Year 1 and Year 2;
- Years 3 and 4;
- Years 5 and 6.

A further division of the aims of teaching gymnastics into four key sub-headings will help teachers to understand where work in this area is focused at particular points and support progression in the work to be covered. If, as suggested here, *body*, *dynamic*, *spatial* and *relationships* are aspects of movement education central to learning in this area, so is a movement vocabulary to support this. These are referenced within the teaching content section of this book and as a further appendix in the materials, and are hugely significant for communicating ideas, setting learning tasks and prompting responses from children, and need to be at the forefront of a teacher's delivery style when teaching gymnastics.

The ideas and structure presented here are models to work from, to refer to when the work needs further consolidation or extension. They match (in six cases) to medium-term planning, again subject to rates of progress. A rationale for the teaching of gymnastics, markers of child development to assist decisions when to teach what, and extension work possibilities, are provided for teacher reference and potential use. The materials also seek to promote confidence in individual teachers' abilities to present work in this area positively, with enthusiasm and effectively, by presenting an increased knowledge base to this particular subject.

They should not be seen in isolation from other resources and support materials. Indeed, the very best practitioners will look for links with other sources of subject knowledge in this sphere and harness what is presented here alongside what they commonly use already. Expanding one's own source of backcloth materials helps to address the alternatives that are on offer and meets much of the demand for ideas and practical solutions to everyday planning concerns.

Teachers are therefore invited to use these materials freely, with their own interpretations, and openly share what they have to offer with others. Do keep in mind the importance of teachers being prepared to repeat and consolidate previous work, to cover tasks and themes that have been covered previously in a variety of different ways and with different approaches. Just such an approach will take account of children's development, their differing growth patterns, the need for provision of work that includes provision for children's developing strength, and also allows for teacher's own personal delivery style to surface. This will entail different task setting in floor work, and alternative ways of teaching through a fuller range of organisational methods on the apparatus (to include different layouts and ways of organising children in their use of portable and fixed equipment). It is the primary aim of these materials that teachers profit from their detail and utilise them accordingly for everyone's benefit.

2 A Rationale for Primary School Gymnastics

The place of gymnastics in a child's education has reached a point where its importance needs to be restated. The primary school has long been the place where the individual child's 'whole education' is looked after, where teachers value the opportunity to see advances in the full range of educational experiences and activities and to witness strides made in intellectual and physical capabilities. Gymnastic activities, as a fundamental part of the physical education curriculum, have traditionally been the area of the curriculum where physical and therefore movement capabilities can be closely witnessed. It is the area where children learn about how their bodies move, what different body parts can do in cooperation with other parts and how their bodies can move in space and in relation to other children. It is also the place where the challenges of working at different speeds, heights and levels and coming into contact with a range of different surfaces occur.

Moreover, the contribution that work in the area makes to learning in other PE areas, like dance and games, is an added consideration to be borne in mind when justifying the importance of gymnastic activities. The development of a movement vocabulary that promotes, for example, a variety of responses to ways of travelling, using space, making different body shapes, balancing on different body parts, jumping and landing skills and working at differing speeds, is very clearly required in the performance aspects of those core PE areas too. Teachers' awareness of the potential for transferability of skill learning will enhance the overall knowledge, skills and understanding referenced as part of National Curriculum PE requirements. It could also be added that as children do acquire greater control, accuracy and versatility in their motor competence, so gymnastics can also bring a discipline to their motor performance.

A rationale for teaching gymnastics in the primary school setting could be summarised as follows:

- *Why?* To service the need for children to become increasingly controlled and skilful in their physical movements and competences. Gymnastics is primarily concerned with both gross and fine motor development and contributes markedly to gradual and progressive improvement in coordination, balance, flexibility, strength and stamina (specifically on improving cardiovascular efficiency).

- *What?* To broaden children's abilities in jumping and landing skills, rolling actions and taking weight on different body parts, and to promote a range of different travelling actions.
- *Where?* The ability to display the broadening range of skills on the floor, initially on low apparatus level surfaces and increasingly on the varied surfaces offered by a full provision of gymnastic apparatus, including apparatus that provides opportunities to work at increased heights.
- *How?* Through a full range of teaching methods and an approach that promotes children succeeding at their own level – using teaching methods that focus on promoting the individual child's learning and success in physical activity.
- *When?* Consistently through well thought through planned units of work over concentrated periods of time, consolidating what has gone before and extending children's repertoire of skilful body actions.

It would be useful to add a further question: what would be the result of children not experiencing this area of learning? It might be appropriate to suggest that if this were the case then a vital cog in children's all round development would be missing, and there would inevitably be a shortfall in their physical performance capabilities. Furthermore, the wider brief of PE should not be understated. The subject generally, and gymnastics specifically, makes a major contribution to speaking and listening skills, children's aesthetic and artistic development and their ability to develop problem-solving skills, as well as nurturing interpersonal and observational skills. These are all invaluable life skills and part and parcel of the wider curriculum.

3 Motor Development

When we identify the notable physical differences between children in the age phase it is very obvious that what marks out children between the ages of five and 11 is their differences in height and weight. However, this is less marked for children between five and seven, and very evident when children begin to sprout in all directions at varying rates across the later childhood period. The work to be covered in gymnastics needs to reflect these physical differences, as well as taking note of the types of activities that promote physical (and therefore motor) development. Table 1 logs typical motor characteristics by age groups and the types of activities that will promote further development.

An ultimate aim of physical education in the primary school is to provide learning opportunities that promote a series of movement activities that continually service the need for improved and increased efficiency in overall motor function in children. This is achieved by the broad and balanced curriculum advocated by National Curriculum PE, includes adherence to individual and group activity across a spectrum of activity and is sequenced to match with the growth and developmental needs of children across the age phase. The ten distinct components of 'efficient motor function' should be embedded within planning considerations, whatever area of PE is intended to be delivered (see below).

Ten distinct components of efficient motor function

1. Symmetrical activity
2. Basic body movement
3. Large muscle development
4. Fine muscle development
5. Eye–hand coordination
6. Eye–foot coordination
7. Body image
8. Balance
9. Rhythm
10. Space and direction

(from Stewart, D. 1990)

Table 1 The development of children from five to 11 years old

Age	Motor/physical development	Activities to promote motor/physical development
Five to six years	They are very energetic. They master skipping and throwing a ball, but not catching it. By this age it is evident whether they are right- or left-handed. At five years old they have poise and good control of their body. They will develop certain interests in sport, dance etc. They might take extra lessons in some of these. The development of physical skill relates closely to the development of personal self-esteem.	Provide gross motor activities with learning skills such as skipping, throwing a ball or dancing. Provide endurance-building activities.
Seven to eight years	Children have slow and steady physical growth. Characteristically they play actively and become more fatigued by sitting for long periods than by physically moving. They play vigorously at one activity, but will quickly drop it for another. They enjoy active games and team sports with an emphasis on skill development and lots of opportunity to practise. They understand and accept rules, but will change them depending on the group. They have a belief in fair play.	Provide opportunities for children to solve problems. Listen and facilitate learning. Provide ideas for further discovery. Provide opportunities for children to create activities, games and stories that stretch their imagination and test ideas. Ensure that children are part of the decision-making process through the use of guided discovery and problem-solving. Provide opportunities for children to skip, run, jump and cycle to assist in the development and practice of new skills. Provide activities that require problem-solving and teamwork. Allow children time to learn skills and practise them. Provide a variety of activities in which the number of participants varies from solitary to team and the skill level changes to include endurance, agility, concentration, coordination and movement. Provide games and sports that focus on enjoyment rather than winning. Give everyone an opportunity to play.
Nine to 11 years	Children consume tremendous energy (and are often hungry). They may give little thought to other bodily needs except when hurt or tired. Body growth slows down until just before puberty, when it accelerates. Girls are 12–15 months ahead in development. Right or left dominance is established and manipulative skills increase. Hand–eye coordination is well developed. Children are now ready for skill building. Late in the phase, boys and girls may be very fidgety and squirmy. Children are generally healthy.	Channel competitive energy into activities that require the group and individuals to do their best and reward success. Praise small victories and slowly build up to larger (or more complex) goals. Encourage 'brainstorming' and creative problem-solving. Provide activities that illustrate the value of people with different skills. Ensure that activities provide for success regardless of physical stage. Games emphasising precise coordination can hurt self-esteem.

4 Ensuring Continuity and Progression in the Work

Teachers will appreciate the need to identify the progression expected across the primary age range, acknowledging where the children to whom they are teaching gymnastic content have come from, and where they need to go to in their learning. The following section describes the type of planning required for each stage of learning across the primary age phase.

The Foundation Stage and Key Stage 1

Being aware of the background of play and movement experience of the children in the early stages is very important. Some children will have attended play group settings or nursery classes which may well have provided a variety of physical experiences, but others may not have benefited from such opportunities and may exhibit a marked lack of physical confidence. The basic work must therefore allow these young children to explore the simple actions of jumping, rolling, balancing and climbing, as well as finding out which parts of the body are needed to support itself when it is still, or which can assist it to move: hands and feet, shoulders, seat etc. During this exploration the children should be made aware of where the body and its constituent parts are moving, whether it is moving on the spot, in the larger area of the hall or on or around apparatus. As the child becomes more skilful he or she should be encouraged to join actions together to form a simple movement phrase or pattern. Initially the children should be restricted to linking two actions that lead smoothly from the first to the second: for example, a jump to land under control, then roll.

The teacher's choice of words, which promote movement responses from the children and need to be understood by them, is of great importance at this stage. The personal vocabularies of children can be increased by their greater appreciation and understanding of the meaning of words that have been used to stimulate, extend and enhance body actions, e.g. moving along, through, up, down, stepping, sliding. Other words may be used that increase children's awareness of space and help them to grasp concepts, e.g. backwards, sideways, behind, forwards, in front of, left, right.

By the end of this stage most children are adventurous and able to move confidently, freely and safely on the floor and on a variety (albeit still relatively low) of apparatus.

Key Stage 2: Years 3 and 4

Much of the material for this stage should reinforce and extend the basic work covered previously. In setting tasks teachers should always refer to specific action words and body parts to achieve a clear response from the children. Greater control and appreciation of body outline should be expected, together with an increased awareness of the movement of other children in close proximity, especially when working on apparatus.

It will be necessary to continue to encourage children to link movements together in simple, yet developing, sequences. A combination of more than three or four actions is likely to be within the capabilities of most children of this age, although there will be marked differences in terms of the continuity achieved, the skill levels attained and the range of actions performed.

When setting tasks on the floor or on the apparatus, the teacher's choice of language continues to be very important. A great deal of the work continues to be exploratory, and quick responses to tasks set for lower juniors are emphasised and encouraged, since too detailed analysis or description of actions can lead to a lack of spontaneity and (potentially) to subsequent boredom. The keynotes in this age group are clearly action, participation and involvement.

Early work with a partner should be carefully considered. Many children do not find it easy to match the movement of others, or to adapt their own ideas to working with someone else. However, working at simple tasks with a partner can be both challenging and enjoyable, and may help some children to clarify their movements and ideas.

This is a period when children should be trained to observe the movement of others. By careful and informed observation they can learn a great deal that will help to improve or add variety to their own work. The ability to observe and extract from what they have seen, what is significant in the movements and actions observed, should be developed by asking children to look for particular features of the work, e.g. what parts of the body are being used to support the weight; at what speed is the body moving; does the body movement change direction during the sequence?

Demonstrations by the teacher or children should be short and used sparingly. The point of any demonstration should be clearly established and positive teaching points made as a result. One further point here: ensure that any demonstrations are within the attainment of the children being taught. Nothing detracts more from potential performance than to see action demonstrated beyond the scope of the majority of children.

Key Stage 2: Years 5 and 6

At this stage children will achieve a higher level of skilful response to tasks set by the teacher provided that the earlier work to develop strength, suppleness and an appreciation of quality of movement has been successfully carried out. The children by this stage should be able to respond to the demands of thoughtful, sustained and concentrated work. Their own choice of actions can be refined to produce movement sequences appropriate to the problems and tasks set by the teacher. Their awareness of body movement should equip them to select actions that flow naturally from one movement to another. An example would be the choice of an appropriate movement to follow an inverted position using the momentum created by overbalancing and controlling and adapting it to produce the next phase of the sequence, e.g. handstand into controlled forward roll.

The ability to observe the work of others should be further developed so that constructive, positive criticism is expected and encouraged in the pursuit of quality work. The exploration of tasks with a partner or in small groups is an important aspect of the work at this stage and may lead to a greater variety of response and a greater appreciation of the needs, strengths and limitations of others. It may also help the less skilful child to work with more confidence.

5 National Curriculum Physical Education

It is worth noting that 'gymnastic activities' feature prominently in both KS1 and KS2 programmes of study in the PE National Curriculum. Of further note is the fact that the importance of PE is hallmarked in National Curriculum documentation by the statement that the subject 'promotes physical skilfulness, physical development and a knowledge of the body in action'. This represents a clear reference to how gymnastic activities particularly service the needs of children in the promotion of these aims. This is further endorsed within the *Curriculum Guidance for the Foundation Stage* (DfEE 2000), where it is stated that:

> **Physical development** [in the foundation stage] is about improving skills of coordination, control, manipulation and movement. Physical development has two other very important aspects. It helps children gain confidence in what they can do and enables them to feel the positive benefits of being healthy and active. Effective physical development helps children develop a positive sense of well-being.
>
> To give all children the best opportunities for effective physical development, practitioners should give particular attention to:
>
> - planning activities that offer appropriate physical challenges;
> - providing sufficient space, indoors and outdoors, to set up relevant activities;
> - giving sufficient time for children to use a range of equipment;
> - providing resources that can be used in a variety of ways or to support specific skills;
> - introducing the language of movement to children alongside their actions;
> - providing time and opportunities for children with physical disabilities or motor impairments to develop their physical skills, working as necessary with physiotherapists and occupational therapists;
> - using additional adult help, if necessary, to support individuals and to encourage increased independence in physical activities.

Using these benchmarks as the building blocks on which to build children's further physical development, the *Physical Education in the National Curriculum* (DfEE 1999) documentation states that:

At Key Stage 1 in Gymnastic activities pupils should be taught to:

   (a) perform basic skills in travelling, being still, finding space and using it safely, both on the floor and using apparatus;

   (b) develop the range of their skills and actions (for example, balancing, taking off and landing, turning and rolling);

   (c) choose and link skills and actions in short movement phrases;

   (d) create and perform short, linked sequences that show a clear beginning, middle and end and have contrasts in direction, level and speed.

At Key Stage 2 in Gymnastic activities pupils should be taught to:

   (a) create and perform fluent sequences on the floor and using apparatus;

   (b) include variations in level, speed and direction in their sequences.

When we look at the level descriptors for meeting PE attainment targets it is clear where the referencing to learning within gymnastic activities appears within the statements. For example, at Level 1,

> Pupils copy, repeat and explore simple skills and actions with basic control and coordination . . . they start to link these skills and actions in ways that suit the activities . . . they describe and comment on their own and others' actions . . . they talk about how to exercise safely, and how their bodies feel during an activity.

At Level 2,

> pupils explore simple skills . . . they copy, remember, repeat and explore simple actions with control and coordination . . . they vary skills, actions and ideas and link these in ways that suit the activities . . . they talk about differences between their own and others' performance and suggest improvement . . . they understand how to exercise safely, and describe how their bodies feel during different activities.

At Key Stage 2, Level 3 descriptors state that

> pupils select and use skills, actions and ideas appropriately, applying them with coordination and control . . . they show that they understand tactics and composition by starting to vary how they respond . . . they can see how their work is similar to and different from others' work, and use this understanding to improve their own performance . . . they give reasons why warming up before an activity is important, and why physical activity is good for their health.

11

At Level 4, the culmination of where the work in all children's PE in primary schools should get to, the descriptors state that

> pupils link skills, techniques and ideas and apply them accurately and appropriately . . . their performance shows precision, control and fluency, and that they understand tactics and composition . . . they compare and comment on skills, techniques and ideas used in their own and others' work, and use this understanding to improve their performance . . . they explain and apply basic safety principles in preparing for exercise . . . they describe what effects exercise has on their bodies, and how it is valuable to their fitness and health.

Of course there will be children in every class who exceed these expectations and those who are still working towards the attainment levels set out in the documentation. What is crucial is for teachers to recognise the important role that gymnastics plays in pursuing an individual response to movement tasks set, and also to have and maintain reasonable expectations of children's abilities to respond naturally and within their capabilities. Taking children to milestones in their physical development is demonstrated through gymnastic activities – providing further challenge to both check and extend their performance levels is the role the teacher needs to play to service these objectives.

6 Developing the Work

Ensuring Progressive Learning

As a starting premise teachers need to acknowledge that children are naturally inclined to be active and, if given the right type of opportunity and encouragement along the way, will develop their motor skills naturally, and pick up on a lot of incidental learning as well. If adequate time, space and apparatus are provided for gymnastic work children will develop their skill, confidence and versatility just by being given such opportunities. If there remains an emphasis on allowing children to make their own discoveries as to what their bodies can do, they will acquire a knowledge about their capabilities, and progress will be marked by increased confidence, greater skill competence and more creativity in their movement. The skill of the teacher is to build on this natural development by giving direction and encouragement to get the children to think imaginatively about their movements. The role of the teacher is all-important in developing the work – he or she can either assist progress or stand in its way.

Basic Tips for Teachers

The individual child, not just those who excel, is the focus of work in this area of the curriculum. Therefore:

- Ensure the aims, intended learning outcomes and theme of each lesson are clear – do not try to cover too much in one session. It is better to consolidate the learning with substance than cover too much ground too quickly.
- Don't get in the way of the children practising and developing their ideas by too much intervention by the teacher.
- On the other hand, too little intervention allows bad habits to develop and does not therefore facilitate the correction of such faults – a careful balance is needed where intervention is concerned.
- Don't expect the same response from all the children to set tasks – allow for individual interpretation and acknowledge individual ability.
- Don't put too much, or too little, emphasis on activity rather than quality in the work – the balance has to be right.

Markers for Progress

If we want children to make the expected progress in this area of the curriculum then the following strategies need to be implemented:

- Consistent and careful planning, preparation and organisation.
- Vitality and enthusiasm generated by the teacher spurs on a keen class and promotes a similar response from children of all abilities and levels of enthusiasm.
- Control and discipline within lessons is important, but should not detract from positive, working atmospheres that are conducive to learning.
- A sound knowledge of movement principles, including how children move characteristically at five as opposed to their abilities at eight and eleven.
- Plenty of opportunity to allow classes to explore and make choices about their movement.
- Injection of praise, encouragement and support – the children will respond to commentary and feedback that display an interest and value in their work.
- Built-in opportunities to enable children to reflect on their work, share their ideas with others and understand why the work is relevant.
- Highlighting of achievement – build on success.

First Gymnastics Lessons with a New Class

The nature of teaching primary aged children brings with it the challenge of meeting a different set of children each year. This means there is a need to inculcate children into the frameworks for delivery that match teachers' individual knowledge, expertise and ways of doing things. The emphasis on such work for them is always high on the agenda in September and October of each school year. This is where gymnastics teaching and learning can greatly assist a teacher in establishing the empathy and class bonding that are so crucial if expectations for a good year are to be met. Early observation of children moving in space, among each other, confronting the challenges of apparatus work, not least in the setting up and dismantling and putting away of the equipment, can tell the teacher a lot about the strategies that will or will not work with his or her new class. The knock-on effect on classroom practice will also benefit relationships and the early establishment of a rapport conducive to maximising the learning potential of the class generally.

A good way to address these concerns is to teach gymnastic activities at the very start of a new year, with some very general activity sessions to give assessment opportunities to the teacher, and therefore, identifying what needs to be covered and from what starting base. The first few lessons of the year with a new class could focus on floorwork, followed by another on simple apparatus set-ups, possibly with another more complex format. The information needed to be able to plan future input should come out of this, and also give a general picture of individual ability.

Demonstration

Although there is no compulsion to use teacher demonstration to show children the skills, actions and movements we want them to master, there is little doubt that this helps in modelling the basics of good performance. There are alternatives – the particularly able child performer, the 'best' attempt at the action demo etc. There is little to be gained by demonstration of a skill, an action or a movement that is beyond the capabilities of the vast majority of the class – this can be off-putting if the skill is too difficult, or too easy. The challenge must suggest that there is a quality to be aimed for that is attainable through practice and over time. It is far better that a teacher presents material to children that teachers acknowledge they are learning too. This shared experience leads to better relationships between the teacher and the class as a whole. This puts all involved in the learning process on an equal footing, ensures that progression is in keeping with the abilities of the class, and in the children's eyes means that teachers are continuing their education at the same time as them. A lot of credibility can be acquired with such an approach and this will further develop the relationship aspects that can be accrued in this area of the curriculum.

Progression

If real progress is to be achieved then individual teacher's planning needs to set out key learning objectives, with attainable assessment criteria that match, to ensure that learning is continuous and progressive. It also clearly needs to match children's capabilities, therefore prompting the need for regular and ongoing recording of children's achievement and attainment. The recognition that progress is only apparent over a period of time, not necessarily from lesson to lesson, is vitally important in this respect. What follow are key markers for teachers to use when assessing progress over time. These are particularly focused on children's performance in a wide-ranging array of features that give clear indications of learning progress *in* and *through* gymnastics.

Assessing progress in gymnastics throughout the primary age phase: 20 key markers

1   *Changing for PE*. Children remember, with less reminding needed, to bring their kit, they change increasingly quickly for lessons and afterwards and there is less fuss and bother with this important feature of PE generally. Children are more concerned with the content of the lesson to follow and look forward to the next one to come as a result of their experiences.

2   *Beginnings of lessons and free choice issues*. Children enter working spaces and have initial tasks to work on immediately. They also display greater independence of thought and action when presented with open-ended choices and tasks.

---

3   *Assembling apparatus.* The children become much more adept in carrying and assembling apparatus, and they do this increasingly speedily and efficiently and with increasing awareness of safety issues.

4   *Learning atmospheres.* Progressively the emphasis is more on quiet, controlled and concentrated work as children become increasingly immersed in the work that is set. The 'sound' of a gymnastics lesson is concerned with moving bodies in space, and safe, controlled and resilient contact with the different surfaces offered by apparatus.

5   *Use of space available.* Children's awareness of the space available, floor and apparatus, becomes more marked in terms of how they use it personally and in sharing and collaboration with others.

6   *Grouping arrangements.* Children learn to work in changing groups, are aware of moving around apparatus stations *en masse*, and can interpret different apparatus layouts according to tasks set. From early experiences of being part of a set group, they are able to cope with working with different children on a regular basis and share with them their ideas, understanding and awareness of safe work, including the erection and dismantling of the full range of apparatus available.

7   *Impact work.* Work is increasingly controlled, resilient and always safe. Eye–foot coordination is at the core of more skilful work, with lightness and 'feel' increasingly to the fore.

8   *Sustained performance.* As energy levels increase children are able to work for longer periods, and can apply greater effort levels to their work. They are constantly 'on the lookout' for places to work, be it on the floor, apparatus or combinations of both; there is a quick start to practice and work; and when they seek out different starting and exit points there is a declining need to queue, particularly with regard to apparatus usage.

9   *Whole body emphasis.* As awareness grows of how the body and its constituent parts move, a greater range of combined actions are used, with an emphasis on using the whole body. Agility and athleticism improve as mobility and increased suppleness become more evident. Extension and tension in body movement and action are increasingly a feature of the work produced.

10   *Creativity and variety.* The work produced displays an all-round improvement in quality as children add changes of direction and speed, work at different levels, follow pathways in their movement that are varied and show differing body shapes in their actions. The continuity and flow of movement reflect the growth in ideas and the individuality to be promoted in response to tasks set and themes being explored.

11   *Understanding and knowledge.* As experience and therefore knowledge develops, the application of previous learning comes increasingly into play as different themes and tasks are presented in the work.

12   *Confidence and self-esteem.* These are best witnessed with children's ability to work at different levels or when the body is upside down, and in skilfully working in close proximity to others. As children become more aware of their capabilities they are increasingly prepared to confront more challenging tasks and to do this with personal drive and determination in order to succeed, ever mindful and conscious of ensuring safety principles in their work.

13   *Performance skill.* Individual skill thresholds rise so that more difficult tasks and more complex series of actions can be achieved. An example is the ability to perform a headstand with legs extended and held for a slow count of three, and to be able to come out of that immediately into a forward roll to a controlled finish.

14 *More precise and defined work*. With younger children the work will emphasise a highly individualised, experimental, free choice set of characteristics. As children become more skilled they will be able to respond to more defined tasks, and work towards more exact performance.

15 *Body control*. Flow of movement and the ability to exert the right level of muscle tension as applicable to a variety of situations is exhibited. General 'body management' is enhanced – children are more in control of their bodies.

16 *Collaboration and cooperation*. The ability to work as an individual, with a partner, in groups, sharing ideas and learning from others, reflects a growth of social skills to be promoted in gymnastics. The sharing of workspace and the need for cooperation when assembling apparatus are two clear examples where this is evidenced, but so is the ability of children to be increasingly able to adapt their own ideas when working with others.

17 *Movement flow*. The increasing ability to devise more complex sequences of movement, and the quality of linking actions ever more smoothly, are developmental characteristics of gymnastics work.

18 *Quality work*. Emphasising the need to plan, practise and modify initial ideas links thought and action requirements. Adding personal style and gloss (or 'flair') is an important part of working towards making the final product – the performance – *quality work*.

19 *Children's attitudes*. Gymnastic activities provide opportunities to develop body skill and therefore confidence and enhanced self-esteem in children. This can be carried over into other learning situations and be exploited further in other curriculum areas. The enthusiasm, willingness to 'have a go', pride in showing good work and confidence accrued over time from success in this area are the hallmarks of a well motivated child.

20 *Key skills enhancement*. Children's key (or core) skills of stability, locomotion and manipulation are greatly enhanced by a continuous, progressive gymnastic programme. There should be discernible progress made in all these areas as children become the more skilled, more competent, motor efficient beings we expect them to be by the time they leave the primary school in readiness for the more defined PE curriculum of the secondary school.

Children tend to produce what is expected of them, and teachers need to ensure they have a clear picture of what can be achieved in gymnastics over time. The setting of high standards, and the demand for children to produce their best efforts at all times, help the individual child to develop as a person as well as someone who is becoming *physically educated*.

Observation and Assessment

An integral assessment tool to be employed by all teachers teaching all aspects of PE is their ability to observe, analyse and evaluate what they see children doing in their lessons. Essentially this can be summarised under four key headings:

1 *Is the class working safely?* With care, under control, in response to tasks set.
2 *Is the class answering the task?* Listening, understanding, appropriateness of response, challenge.
3 *How well is the task being answered?* Appropriateness of the idea(s), quality of performance.
4 *How can the teacher help?* Feedback and further guidance, clarification, teaching points, demonstration, discussion, suggestion, praise, encouragement, criticism, reflection on the effort.

The above can lead to an overall evaluation of performance out of the observation, and the interpretation and assessment of how the individual child has met the aims of the lesson or overall learning objectives. This leads quite naturally into informing where work needs to go next for the class as a whole, sets up planning the content of the follow-up lesson and can also identify particular tasks for individual children that will progress their learning specifically.

Keeping Records

Recording and keeping written records of children's performances on a regular basis helps teachers to keep track of coverage of the work undertaken and also provides the detail of individual performance over time. This can ultimately lead to summative commentaries on the individual pupil, and set the markers for future planning and for where the work in the area needs to progress to next. Record sheets are a useful mechanism for this (see Appendix 1), but these need to be both manageable and appropriate for the purposes they serve.

Teachers are well aware of the importance of keeping records, not just to help them with future planning, but also as testimony to their provision of quality learning experiences. They also serve the practical purpose of informing end-of-year reporting procedures. On a week-to-week or lesson level, in terms of recording class (and individual children's) performances the following markers are suggested:

- Have a clear picture of what you want to assess. Is it the class as a whole, individuals, particular skills, the response generally to tasks set?
- Identify which children you wish to focus on for recording purposes. Make this manageable, say no more than four or five children each session, enabling coverage of the whole class across a (say) seven-week period (which may well tie in with a specific unit of work).
- Keep a general record of what is covered in a session, as well as notes on the particular children chosen for observation.
- Make reference in your records, where relevant, of organisation, who worked with whom, which groups worked on which apparatus etc.
- If it helps use a template under three headings: 'what the children learnt' 'what I learnt', 'where the work goes next'.

What is advocated here is a procedure to follow for *all* PE lessons, so that the overall picture of children's physical development, competence and skill levels is mapped. From this base a fully informed, and therefore accurate, analysis of how children have performed across the year is achieved, and this supports feedback to colleagues for future reference, parents and the children themselves.

Links with Other Work

Cross-curricular perspectives are an essential consideration when teachers are planning for gymnastic teaching. However, this should not be tokenistic, contrived or artificially construed. The language elements are crucial to delivery: for example, action words that can evoke movement response, naming of body parts, what apparatus is properly called and how we can design interesting apparatus layouts to suit skills development. Bringing learning accrued from other curriculum areas 'to life' is where gymnastics can score heavily in developing and widening knowledge and understanding initially (but not always) gleaned elsewhere. For example, the words 'sequencing' and 'symmetry', which will have emerged in maths work, will have a different meaning when applied to movement, particularly in a gymnastic sense. Individual teachers' ability to respond to such possibilities in their teaching maximise their effectiveness and acknowledge through such an approach their own skill in educating the 'whole' child – an opportunity not to be missed.

There exist plenty of opportunities to bring together work in the classroom with the work to be covered in gymnastics and PE lessons as a whole. Whether it be through the use of music or elements of drama to act as a stimulus for work, or a simple child self-assessment of performance through picture and word format, the possibilities are endless. Consolidation of knowledge and understanding should be at the forefront of thinking and delivery here, utilising the concept of educating the 'whole' child through different means. That action and movement take place, and are immediately evident to the observer, makes this area of the curriculum significantly distinct and therefore flexible in the way learning takes place – a benefit to reap for many other subject areas in the primary curriculum.

Extracurricular Work: The School Gym Club

Where this is possible such provision should be available to all children who have an interest in developing further the work that is covered in normal lessons. How far the work can be extended will very much be dictated by the knowledge base and expertise of the teachers prepared to make such provision. If the teacher has been the recipient of further training and personal coaching in the area then the possibilities are marked. On the other hand, it should not be thought that such work cannot be done by the motivated (and enthused) practitioner who wishes merely to provide extra provision to move individuals' learning and performance levels forward. This is very much the case at primary level and is a practice to be commended. That it might also lead to further training, as part of ongoing professional development, can only be of benefit longer term.

An important consideration when providing these opportunities is to be consistent with the regularity of these club-type activities – nothing is more dispiriting for children than to be offered an activity that only takes place at irregular intervals or, worse, that does not take place at all. Careful consideration of why such provision is desirable, with clear intention and purpose in play, and a full commitment to regular delivery, should be uppermost when making such decisions.

The British Gymnastics Association provides excellent support materials to help this work, including proficiency awards that can bolster interest and performance standards. These should be seen as having potential for curriculum time provision as well as in the gym club, and can act as an extra motivational tool for children to work to raise their overall achievement in gymnastics. The idea of inter-school gymnastics festivals and (potentially) competition is a further extension of the work that can result from a whole-school approach to gymnastics provision.

The Next Stage: Secondary School Gymnastics

The work and progress expected at 11 plus will clearly be determined by what has happened previously. The demands of Key Stage 3 ask pupils to be able to:

1. Create and perform complex sequences on the floor and using apparatus.
2. Use techniques and movement combinations in different gymnastic styles.
3. Use compositional principles when designing their sequences (for example, changes in level, speed, direction and relationships with apparatus and partners).

The keynote here for teachers teaching at primary level is to bear this in mind when planning an appropriate gymnastics curriculum for pupils in readiness for the demands that they will face when entering secondary education. Children who leave their primary school with confidence in their movement abilities, and have at their disposal sound stability, locomotor and manipulative, skills will prosper from the typical PE curriculum to be offered at 11 plus.

7 A Checklist for Health and Safety in Gymnastic Activities

Teaching area

- Sufficient space available and conducive to the whole age range (older children take up more space).
- Clean floor area and clean equipment (particularly surfaces) to be used.
- Be aware of exit doors, windows, window sills, radiators, other (unrelated) equipment and furniture (including shelving) in the workspace.

Clothing and jewellery

- Children *and* teachers need to change into suitable clothing that allows for safe and efficient movement (including shirts tucked into shorts).
- Long hair needs to be tied back.
- Jewellery needs to be removed (ever mindful of cultural diversity).
- Bare foot work should be encouraged (clean surfaces permitting!). This promotes lightness in movement, sensitivity to different surfaces and the opportunity to show extension and tension in movement.

Equipment

- Needs to be safe, clean, taken out and stored correctly and in the same place.
- Should be called by its appropriate name (whole-school policy issue).
- Needs to be regularly maintained (once a year) by specialist contractors.
- Children need to be taught how to handle, retrieve, carry and place equipment from as early a point in their gymnastics learning as possible.
- Mats should be located where *anticipated* landings are expected.
- Jumping and landing skills (on to and off different surfaces) need to be taught.
- Teachers *and* children check linked equipment, bolts, pulley fastenings etc. *before* work commences.
- Children *never* sit on apparatus when tasks are being set for the class – this should include mats to retain consistency of approach.

Warm up and cool down

- Apply in every lesson. Link it to the main input but try to include a balance of activities that contrast with the main lesson themes.

Children

- Understand and readily respond to agreed start and stop signals.
- Are taught to take increasing responsibility for both themselves and others.
- Build on knowledge and experience.
- Understand safety aspects and routines to follow.
- Are all included, *including* those not taking an active part in the lesson.

Miscellaneous

- Do not use whistles in gymnastics sessions. Use the voice as the communication tool.
- Work to avoiding queuing, particularly for apparatus work. Encourage children to 'look for other places to work'. Keep general levels of activity across the class high.
- Include commentary to children. Provide ongoing feedback to individuals, groups and the class as a whole, and maintain an overview of the whole class *as they work*.
- Be mobile throughout the lessons, maintaining sight of all the children. Establish appropriate teaching positions for whole-class formal input.
- Ensure first aid is readily available and accessible, and that procedures for administering it are known.

Remember: 'There should not be over-reaction to the need for safety. Over-protective teachers and under-challenged lessons are not likely to produce good physical education' (BAALPE 1999).

Endnote

The creation of a safe and positive learning environment in PE generally takes time and, as in the classroom itself, good working routines need to be taught – they don't just happen.

8 Gymnastics Teaching Material for Reception, Year 1 and Year 2

Themes

1 Space
2 Using apparatus
3 Movement tasks
4 Supporting body weight
5 Transference of weight

6 Travelling
7 Lifting body parts high
8 Feet together and apart
9 Curling and stretching

Theme 1: Space

Learning to share space safely

One of the essential and key aims of work with a very young class will be to see that the children allow themselves sufficient space in which to work. This concerns the space they work in as individuals and how that impacts on the space that they share with others. This is crucial learning that will impact on all later work. The teacher will also be concerned with safety and general response, but without lessening the children's sense of exploration, adventure and pleasure from movement opportunity. Children's ability to be creative, individual and naturally responsive to particular tasks set will be a focus of this work.

Warm up activities
- Quiet running, on the spot.
- Quiet running, without touching others.
- Quiet running, stopping on a given signal in a free space.
- Quiet running on the balls of the feet.

Floor work
Whole body work
- Run to a space and, on a given signal, make yourself as small as possible.
- Run to a space and, on a given signal, make yourself as big as possible.
- Provide some 'mini-apparatus' spread across the floorspace: cones, hoops, skittles, discs, skipping-ropes etc. Run past, over or round the apparatus without touching it (or each other).

Lower body work
- Find different ways of travelling to a new space on your feet: skip, jump, hop, gallop, leap etc.
- Run to a new space and, on a given signal, do a big jump.
- Run freely and without touching others change direction on given signal.

Upper body work
- Find different ways of moving with hands and feet touching the floor.
- Move forwards, backwards and sideways, with hands and feet on the floor – facing the ceiling, then facing the floor.
- Put your hands on the floor and take up a small space, then a big space.

Apparatus work (use low level apparatus – mats, benches, box tops, low nesting tables, planks, etc)
- Find different ways of getting on and off the apparatus without touching one another.
- Get on the apparatus at one place, then off at another. Avoid touching other children as you do so.
- Find a place on the apparatus where you can make yourself as big as possible, then another where you can make yourself as small as possible. See if you can hold a position of 'stillness' for a count of three.

Cool down activity (on the floor)
In your own space:
- Try to spread yourself over as much space as possible close to the floor.
- Try to occupy as small a space as possible close to the floor.

Theme 2: Using Apparatus

Learning to use apparatus safely

In the early stages it is crucial to allow time for children to become familiar with the range of apparatus they will confront through their gymnastics work. There is no need to introduce all of this at once. It is better to do this over time, with new apparatus being introduced at irregular intervals to inject more excitement and interest, and therefore more possible applications to their movement. They will need to become aware of the variety of apparatus available, its different textures and surfaces, the way in which it can be gripped, how to get on and off and how it needs to be shared with others in the class. The early experience of handling the different apparatus as well as using it for their gymnastics is all part of the learning to be derived here. Suggestions follow for helping children to explore the possibilities presented by a range of different and varied apparatus.

Using apparatus

OLSON LIBRARY
NORTHERN MICHIGAN UNIVERSITY
MARQUETTE, MI 49855

Small apparatus work
Hoops, skipping ropes, mats, canes, cones, disc markers, skittles placed on the ground (one piece of small apparatus for each child placed in a space)
- Find different ways of going over your apparatus.
- Show different ways of jumping around your apparatus.
- Show a stretched action over your apparatus, then a curled action. Repeat to show another stretch and another curled action.
- Move over your apparatus by placing your hands on the ground.
- Practise approaching and leaving your apparatus from different directions. Can you do it slow, then fast? Can you use your hands in the actions you choose?

Canes, hoops and skipping-ropes supported on skittles or cones
(no touching of the apparatus in any of these activities)
- Find ways of moving over and around your apparatus.
- Make bridge-like shapes over the apparatus – try to hold them for 3 seconds.
- Move under the apparatus, touching the floor with different parts of the body – repeat and touch the floor with other parts of the body.
- Move under the apparatus, making yourself as small as possible, and over the apparatus, making yourself as big as possible.
- Try to keep moving continuously over, under, round the apparatus in different ways, using different body parts.

Large apparatus work (climbing frames, A-frames, linked pieces, etc)
- Run in the spaces, under, round and through the apparatus – don't touch its surfaces.
- On a given signal, stop and grip the nearest apparatus with the hands, climb on slowly without touching other children.
- Climb freely, climb off safely on a given signal.
- Free use of apparatus with continuous movement, using lots of different body parts.
- Find different ways of getting on to the apparatus and different ways of getting off safely.

Apparatus tasks
- Climb freely on the climbing frame, using hands and feet only.
- Find different ways of hanging from the apparatus by hands only.
- Find different places to be curled up and places to be stretched out.
- Climb up the apparatus, then along and down. Can you do the same but 'across' the apparatus?

Benches and mats
- Jump from the bench or mat with a deep, safe landing.
- Move over the mat, through the bench and back over the bench, touching with as many different parts of the body as possible.

- Move along the bench on hands and feet only, first facing the bench and then with your head facing towards the ceiling.
- Put hands on the bench top and jump the feet across from one side to the other. Move down the bench, at different speeds, doing this, and then roll out onto the mat.

Inclined/sloping bench, box (top section only) and mat
- Climb over the box and get off quietly, slowly and safely on to the mat.
- Move up the bench on hands and feet, climb down from the box. Can you do this differently?
- Climb on to the box, slide down the bench on a large part of your body.
- Get on to the apparatus touching first with parts of the body other than the feet. Come off with a jump.
- Repeat but first with parts of the body other than the hands.

Trestles, planks, and mat
- Repeat tasks similar to the above.

Ropes, ladders and trapeze
- Grip the apparatus tightly and try to lift the feet off the ground.
- Try to hang from the apparatus, using hands only.
- Make different patterns with the legs while hanging from the apparatus.
- Grip two different pieces of apparatus (e.g. two ropes, or one rope and an adjacent beam) and repeat the above tasks. Can you use one set of hands with a foot only?

Nesting and agility tables, stools, box tops
- Find ways of getting on using hands and feet only. Come off with a high jump.
- Get on touching with different parts of the body. Come off using hands to take the weight first. Repeat and do differently.

Further opportunities to extend the range of usage of apparatus can be suggested by asking the children to think in the following terms
- Moving around the apparatus on different body parts, in different directions, at different speeds.
- Ways of getting on the apparatus.
- Ways of getting off the apparatus.
- Moving under the apparatus.
- Moving over the apparatus.
- Moving along the apparatus.
- Climbing or jumping up onto the apparatus.
- Climbing or jumping down from the apparatus – safely.

Teachers need to consider within this theme where opportunities arise for children to learn the basics of lifting, carrying and potentially linking different pieces of apparatus. Work on correct lifting techniques can be broached here: 'bending legs, not backs . . . grasping basics . . . cooperating with others to manoeuvre equipment' etc. can all be first addressed quite informally here, building good habits from the beginning. With the teacher's guidance good habits can be nurtured from these starting points.

Cool down activity
- Mirror individually correct lifting techniques. Visualise heavier loads and work with a partner.

Theme 3: Movement Tasks

Learning more movement skills

Here the work is concerned with movements and actions that children perform naturally in their everyday lives and therefore bring to their learning in PE generally. Therefore, activities that involve travelling in different ways, using different parts of their bodies to move from place to place, momentary and more prolonged stillness, jumping and landing skills and their application to work on apparatus are the focus of this particular theme of work.

Warm up activities
- Find different and varied ways of travelling about the hall on the feet. Encourage lightness, free choice of direction and awareness of others.
- Use different parts of the body to move around the space. Can you use your knees, feet and hands, backs and fronts, other parts to move (forwards, backwards, sideways)?

Floor work
Whole body work
- Curl up very small and find different parts of the body that can touch the floor in this position.
- Roll along the floor while curled up as tightly as possible.
- Stretch out and find body parts, big and small, on which you can balance – hold the position for a count of 3.
- Roll along the floor while stretched out (long or wide).

Lower body work
- Practise a variety of ways of moving on your feet: run, walk, hop, skip, jump, gallop, leap (stop on given signal).
- Show how high you can jump and try to land back where you started. (Teach *safe landings*: land on two feet, weight on the balls of the feet, knees forward and feet fairly close together, back straight, ankles and knees bent to absorb the weight, and then extend again to the upright position, with a 'springy' jump and landing.)
- Spring from one foot to the other on the spot: forwards, to the side, backwards, diagonally.
- Jump in different directions. Work on springy jumps to gain height.

Upper body work
- Move about the floorspace on hands and feet.
- Balance on two hands and two feet, two hands and one foot, one hand and two feet, other variations.
- Put your hands on the floor and jump your feet from side to side, forwards and backwards, variations.
- Put your hands on the floor and, keeping your arms straight, jump your feet into the air ('bunny jumps'). Can you get one foot higher than the other, up at the same time, lasting a little longer in the air each time?

Apparatus work
Benches and mats
- Practise different ways of jumping and landing, balancing, rolling, taking weight on hands using the surfaces and floorspace around the apparatus.

Full apparatus
- Move on the apparatus using hands and feet only. Can you keep the movement going 'non-stop'?
- Find ways of supporting yourself on the apparatus and being still (don't hold the still positions for longer than three seconds).
- Find a variety of places on the apparatus where you can hang or swing – safely.
- Find places where you can leave the apparatus with a safe jump and a 'springy' landing.

Other possibilities within this theme
- Ways of moving from one spot or starting place. Travel (walk, run, hop, skip, gallop, roll, jump, swing, heave etc.). Return to the same spot.
- Ways of staying on the same spot.
- Leave the ground or apparatus surface without using the feet: spring from hands only, from a roll, from a balance.
- Landing on body parts other than the feet.
- Taking weight on hands using apparatus surfaces to help to support the action.

Cool down activity
- Choose your best (and quietest) way of moving and travel for 10 seconds from the word 'go' to when you hear 'stop'.

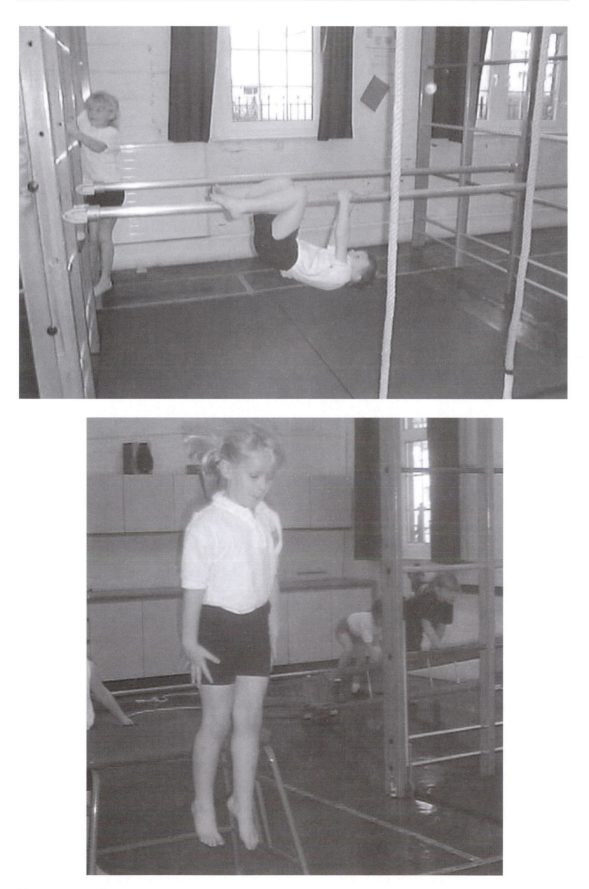

Movement tasks

A unit of work for Key Stage 1 gymnastics: 'Movement tasks'

Year: Reception/1	Key Stage: 1	Time (no. of lessons): six sessions (approx. 35 min each)	Title of unit: 'Movement tasks'	Learning outcome: To build on natural movement actions and apply to apparatus	Cross-curricular elements: Building a movement vocabulary; problem-solving skills; PSHE

Lesson focus on	Lesson 1 Whole body parts	Lesson 2 Large body parts	Lesson 3 Combining movement actions	Lesson 4 Joining up movements	Lesson 5 Groupwork	Lesson 6 Performance
Warm up/introduction	Free movement in large space, then confined spaces. No touching allowed. Maintain movement.	'Move and stop' work, holding very still on stop signal. Using different parts of the body to move.	Jog around the floorspace. On signal, pause, perform a slow roll of choice and continue out of roll back into jog. Be aware of others as you move on foot and through rolling actions.	Spread 'mini-apparatus' and mats across floorspace. Move in and out and around the equipment. On signal touch surface of apparatus with different body parts (a foot, an elbow, a knee, a finger). Repeat and continue.	Number each member of the class as 1, 2, 3 or 4. On call of that number repeat jumping patterns around the space (jump, land, pause; jump, land, pause etc.) until next number is called. Repeat. Encourage observation, response, individuality of movement action.	Working in pairs, one takes a balance position, the other travels around (possibly underneath), towards, away from etc., using a series of movements of choice. Rotate roles.
Floor work	Experiment with different speeds, movement on foot in different directions. *Big* steps, *little* steps, light and heavy. Work on 'sharing' the space available with others moving at the same time.	Rolling actions: mat work (sharing with a partner). Practise different rolls (sideways, forwards, backwards, circular) from corner to corner, using width and length. Work on varying speed and control.	Practise joining balances and rolling actions (working on mats and mini-apparatus). Explore what comes best first to improve links. Show your partner. Copy your partner.	Individually, practise jumps, rolls, simple balances in and around the apparatus. Begin to join these up.	Six areas allocated. Work on practising rolling actions and balances around each other in the space allocated.	Joining movements: add changes of speed and direction. Try to add a change of level to the movements performed.
Apparatus work	Using mini-apparatus make a pathway to follow on the floor. Explore moving around, over, under, away from, towards. Begin to use hands and feet combinations, and other body parts.	Rolling actions: mats and mini-apparatus. Work on stretch, extension, tuck and curled rolls as work progresses on, around, across, under and between the different apparatus.	Introduce low level apparatus (benches, low tables, planks, box sections). Repeat the above.	Organise six apparatus areas. Choose pieces to join up jumps, rolls and balances.	Add apparatus to areas. All starting from different points, practise joining continuous jumps, rolls and balances. No contact allowed with others in the group.	Six apparatus areas. Choose the starting and finishing points and move along the pathway using combinations of jumps, rolls and balances. Repeat and improve.

Concluding activity	Practise your favourite movements. Can you work at different levels (low, medium and high) around the pathways of the mini-apparatus?	Choose your best roll(s) and show (half the class performing and half watching). Reverse and invite comments and 'things to work on next week'.	With a hoop each, practise jumping actions: in and out, across, away from, towards. Bend knees on take off *and* landing. Experiment with one-foot and two-foot take-off and landing.	Arrange the class into groups. Number the members of the groups. Select a number (i.e. one from each group) to show the whole class the actions performed on their set of apparatus. Invite comments.	Each group shows a combined response to the above, with all starting at the same time. Invite comments, compliments and 'things to work on'.	Individualise for demonstration. Highlight qualitative elements and invite feedback from observers. Record individual performance where applicable.
Relationships	Individual and shared	Individual and pairs	Individual and pairs	Individual and groups	Individual and groups	Individual

Resources needed

- Mini-apparatus: cones, canes, skittles, skipping ropes, hoops, bean bags etc.
- Mats, benches, planks, box sections etc.
- Class recording sheets.

For further development of this theme see 'Movement tasks' in the main text.

Attainment Targets: level descriptions 1 and 2

Level 1. 'Pupils copy, repeat and explore simple skills and actions with basic control and coordination. They start to link these skills in ways that suit the activities. They describe and comment on their own and others' actions. They talk about how to exercise safely, and how their bodies feel during an activity.'

Level 2. 'Pupils explore simple skills. They copy, remember, repeat and explore simple actions with control and coordination. They vary skills, actions and ideas and link these in ways that suit the activities. They begin to show some understanding of . . . basic compositional ideas. They talk about differences between their own and others' performance and suggest improvements. They understand how to exercise safely, and describe how their bodies feel during different activities.'

Criteria for assessing attainment

- Class working safely: control.
- Class answering task: listening, responding.
- Quality produced in response to task.
- Response to teaching.
- Ability to work with others.
- Improving accuracy and range of movement.
- Increased imaginative/creative performance.
- Ability to do more than one thing at a time.
- Sustained participation.

General physical requirements across all key stages

Pupils should be taught to:

- To be physically active, adopt good posture.
- To develop flexibility and muscular strength.
- To develop positive attitudes.
- To ensure safe practice.

POS Key Stage 1: NC 1a, b, 2a, b, 3a, b, c, 4a, b

Pupils should be taught to:

- Acquire and develop skills.
- Select and apply skills, tactics and compositional ideas.
- Evaluate and improve performance.
- Acquire knowledge and understanding of fitness and health.

POS (activity specific): NC 8a, b, c, d

Pupils should be taught to:

- Perform basic skills in travelling, being still, finding space and using it safely, both on the floor and using apparatus.
- Develop the range of their skills and actions.
- Choose and link skills and actions in short movement phrases.
- Create and perform short, linked sequences that show a clear beginning, middle and end and have contrasts in direction, level and speed.

Theme 4: Supporting Body Weight

Learning to control growing bodies

It is important from an early stage of work in this area to provide children with many opportunities to experience taking their weight safely on different parts of the body and to control movement and their momentum (and balance) as they do so. This theme accounts for the changing growth patterns prevalent in young children and builds on previous work that will have provided the basis of increased competence and confidence in their abilities. They will be ready for this work if this has been established.

Warm up activities
- Practise different ways of jumping on the spot.
- Move about the whole floorspace with two feet together. Do this in an upright and then a squat position.

Floor work
Whole body work
- Weight on feet only. Lower to touch the floor lightly with a range of body parts, returning to a standing start position.
- Slowly curl up and roll to bring the feet to a new place, and repeat.
- Jump to land on two feet, lower and roll – reverse the pattern.
- Curl up, roll and stop in a balance on different parts of the body.
- Balance on matching parts of the body: knees, shoulders, elbows, tummies, bottoms.
- Balance on two (or more) different parts of the body: one hand and one foot; knees and head; one hand, one foot and an elbow etc.

Lower body work
- Jump to land on two feet or on one foot – for height and for distance.
- Run, jump and stop with a light landing – count to 3 before repeating.
- Jump in different directions and land lightly – again, count to 3 before beginning again.

Upper body work
- Take weight on hands, kick legs up one at a time to land back on the floor lightly.
- Repeat above. Try to bring both feet back to the floor together.
- Balance on hands and feet facing the floor, with back towards floor, with side towards floor – hold each for a count of 3.
- Travel on hands and feet jumping forward, backwards, sideways in turn.

Apparatus work
- Arrive on the apparatus in different ways, onto different body parts, safely.
- Grip the apparatus with hands, feet, knees, other parts – different combinations.
- Hang from different parts of the body – combinations of feet and hands.

- Find places on the apparatus where you can balance. Work on holding for three seconds.

Cool down activity

- Show your best balance on a big part(s) and a small part (s). Hold the stillness for the teacher's count of three.

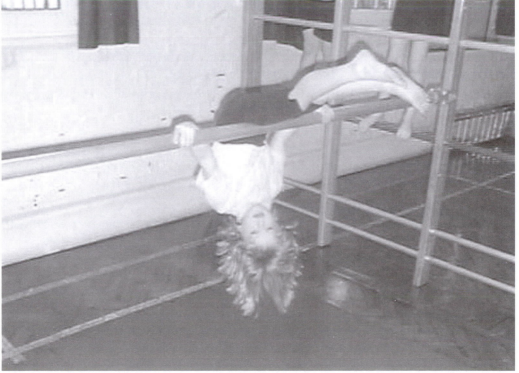

Supporting body weight

Theme 5: Transference of Weight

Learning to take body weight in different positions

As a progression from the previous theme, this particular one takes account of the fact that any movement involves a transference of body weight. Children are used to doing this quite naturally in their everyday movement, but experience and skill need to be developed for the more challenging and difficult situations presented by the apparatus. The emphasis on *how* the body moves between different points of support, aiming therefore to identify and clarify different ways of transferring weight, and thus to improve skill by practising the movement involved, is the key to what is involved in this theme. This theme also involves locomotion, but while locomotion emphasises travel between two points, weight transference emphasises the bodily movements between two weight bearing positions.

Warm-up activities
- Practise a favourite movement on the floor that you have enjoyed doing in a previous lesson.
- Try to include a pattern that involves movement on a big part of the body and then on a small part.

Floor work
Whole body work
- Move your weight from one body part to another: from shoulders to seat; from knees to chest; from hip to hip.
- Find ways of balancing on one body part and then moving to balance on another part.
- Find different ways of rocking the body: on the front; on the back; from side to side.
- Show a shape (long, wide, stretched) on any part of the body, then slowly curl up and roll.

Lower body work
- In an upright position transfer the weight from: one foot to the other; one foot to two feet; two feet to one foot; two feet to two feet; one foot to the same foot.
- Combine the actions above with jumping skills and patterns: forwards; backwards; sideways.

Upper body work
- Transfer weight from feet to hands and hands to feet. Take this into a travelling movement that is continuous around the floorspace.
- In a space of your own, place hands on the floor and keep the head looking at the floor. Try to take weight on your hands by kicking up one leg after the other or by jumping up both feet together (bring feet down lightly, quietly and safely).

Apparatus work
- Find different parts of the body which will support body weight. Choose one, then try to change to a different part.
- Try to get on the apparatus: feet first; hands first; taking weight first of all on a different part of the body (e.g. knees, tummy, bottom).
- Come off the apparatus: hands first; touching with a part of the body first other than feet or hands.
- Transfer the weight of the body from one part to another: feet to hands; hands to another part of the body; one part of the body to another.

Links with other themes
- Transferring weight moving in different *directions*, and at different *speeds*.
- Transferring weight when *curled*, *stretched*, *twisting* or *turning*.

Cool down activity
- Choose two movements. Join them together using a combination of different large and small body parts and surfaces.

Theme 6: Travelling

Learning to increase ways of moving through floor space and on apparatus

Once children are able to transfer their body weight increasingly competently and confidently, they should be encouraged to explore the multitude of ways of travelling and moving their body weight to expand their individual repertoire of different physical movements and actions. This theme may be conveniently introduced with small or mini-apparatus or with just benches and mats and other similar low-level apparatus, with a view to progressing the work to larger apparatus eventually to test similar or different tasks and skills.

Warm up activities
- See how many different ways you can find of supporting your body on the floor – apply a 3 second hold rule for each example.
- Change from one to the next quickly. Progress to one quick, one slow, one quick or vice versa.

Floor work
Whole body work
- Show ways of rolling over the floor when: curled up; stretched out. Vary speed and direction.
- Roll when curled up: sideways; forwards; over one shoulder; backwards.
- Find other ways of travelling on different parts of the body around the floorspace, e.g. sliding, rocking, pushing, pulling.

Lower body work
- Travel around the whole floorspace by: walking; running; hopping; galloping; striding; stepping; springing; skipping – change on given signal.
- Travel with weight high in the air by: jumping; leaping – work on light landings.
- Run, jump and go on running on landing – regain balance before continuing.
- Run, jump and stop with a light landing. Wait for 'go' signal before continuing.

Upper body work
- Put hands on the floor, jump or spring legs into the air and bring them down in a new place, lightly and under control.
- Travel springing between hands and feet. How much floorspace can you cover in the time given? Be aware of others as you move.

Apparatus work (portable and fixed)
- Travel on different parts of the body over apparatus provided.
- Find places on the apparatus that allow you to travel by: jumping; swinging; rolling.
- Travel on different parts of the body from one piece of apparatus, over the floor to new apparatus, and continue over the range of apparatus provided.
- Travel using one part to support your weight: feet; hands; body.

Links with other themes
- Travel *slowly*, then *quickly*, sometimes pausing between movements.
- Travel with *different body parts high* – e.g. where the head is lower than other body parts.

Cool down activity
- Join two favourite ways of travelling: one fast, one slow. Include definite start and finish positions.

Travelling

A unit of work for Key Stage 1 gymnastics: 'Travelling'

Year: 2	Key Stage: 1	Time (no. of lessons): six sessions (approx. 35 min each)	Title of unit: 'Travelling'	Learning outcome: To explore further ways of travelling and propelling body weight	Cross-curricular elements: Continuing to build a movement vocabulary; problem-solving skills; PSHE

	Lesson 1 Whole body parts	Lesson 2 Use of large and small body parts	Lesson 3 Large body actions	Lesson 4 Moving continuously	Lesson 5 Groupwork	Lesson 6 Performance and assessment
Lesson focus on						
Warm up/introduction	Practise quiet walking, jogging, running in different directions. Listen for 'stop' signal and hold 'still' position, and make sure nobody is near you.	'Move and stop' work. Use different parts of the body to move around the floorspace. On 'stop' signal make a big, small or twisted shape in your own space. Repeat and perform contrasting actions on stop signal.	Move around the whole floorspace in different directions (forwards, backwards, sideways). Maintain a constant space between each other. Achieve 'stillness' on given signal. 'What is your space when "still" like?'	Travel on floor from feet to hands to feet in various directions. Work on facing the floor (prone) and facing the ceiling (supine).	Hopping and skipping actions. Combine with a follow-up jump and landing that ends in 'stillness' or regained balance. (Work on feet together and apart. What's best?) Repeat, landing on hands, then feet, and add changes of speed and direction. Practise improving the landing (hold for a count of three before repeating).	Teacher directed. Individually travel around the floorspace and on command perform a different shape: long, wide, tucked, near to the floor, away from the floor etc.
Floor work	Travelling using feet only: walking, skipping, hopping, running, moving on the spot and around the floorspace in different directions.	Explore travelling in a variety of ways: on hands and feet, bouncing with feet together and apart, with hands close together and further apart. Develop to travel in different directions: forwards, backwards, sideways.	Travel on large body parts. Explore ways of travelling on tummy, back, bottom, sides. Watch each other (half the class watch, half show, then reverse roles).	Travel continuously on tummy and back. Turn from one to the other using sliding and rolling actions. Add stretching out long and tucking up as the travel continues.	In pairs, on and around mats only, practise sliding and rolling actions using different body parts. Watch and try to copy. Put together a minimum of three consecutive movements or actions.	Choose different ways of jumping and landing. Add shapes to the point of flight achieved. Build to include a follow-up action on landing, e.g. a roll or sliding action close to the floor surface. Repeat.
Apparatus work	Using mini-apparatus, travel along or around the rope, skip and hop into and out of the hoops. Link movements: run, skip, hop, jump into and out of the hoop, over the rope. Add cones, canes, skittles and bean bags as floor obstacles.	Experiment with different ways of travelling along, over, across and underneath benches and mats, e.g. with both hands, one hand only, bouncing, hopping, skipping, walking and using combinations of hands and feet.	Introduce low level linked apparatus (benches, low tables, box sections, A frames). Try out new ideas and skills to move on, along, across and underneath the apparatus. Show a partner your movement and actions. Try to copy/mirror.	Organise six apparatus group areas. Travel along surfaces and link rolling actions. Look for different points to get on and off the apparatus surfaces using similar travelling actions.	Six full apparatus areas for groups. Show travel along, on over, across, underneath, through, between, up down etc. Use the full range of previously practised movements and actions. Rotate groups at least once on to a different set of apparatus.	Full apparatus set up (six areas). Repeat the task above, now applied to the apparatus. Set task to move continuously across the whole apparatus, showing full range of movements and actions, different shapes, speed, direction, level etc. Rotate to another area and repeat.

Concluding activity	Walking or light jogging. Quiet work stretching out wide and up high as travel happens. Control with teacher signals.	On signal, walk quietly, slowly and lightly to a space and curl up as small as possible. Repeat to make as large a shape as possible.	Find a floorspace. Lie on your front or back. Stretch out in a long or wide position. Curl up small and tight. Release slowly and repeat.	Arrange the class into groups. Number the members of the groups. Select a number (i.e. one from each group) to show the whole class the actions performed on their set of apparatus. Invite comments.	Each group shows a combined response to the above, with all starting at the same time. Invite comments, compliments and 'things to work on'.	Individualise for demonstration. Highlight qualitative elements and invite feedback from observers. Final activity in floorspace: from a tight, curled up position unwind very slowly to as wide and pointed a position as possible. Hold the final position for a count of three.
Relationships	Individual and shared	Individual, pairs and groups	Individual and pairs	Individual and groups	Individual and groups	Individual and groups

Resources needed

- Mini-apparatus: cones, canes, skittles, skipping ropes, hoops, bean bags etc.
- Mats, benches, planks, box sections, nesting tables, climbing frames etc.
- Class recording sheets.

For further development of this theme see 'Travelling' in the main text.

General physical requirements across all key stages

- To be physically active, adopt good posture.
- To develop flexibility and muscular strength.
- To develop positive attitudes.
- To ensure safe practice.

Attainment Targets: level descriptions 1 and 2

Level 1. 'Pupils copy, repeat and explore simple skills and actions with basic control and coordination. They start to link these skills in ways that suit the activities. They describe and comment on their own and others' actions. They talk about how to exercise safely, and how their bodies feel during an activity.'

Level 2. 'Pupils explore simple skills. They copy, remember, repeat and explore simple actions with control and coordination. They vary skills, actions and ideas and link these in ways that suit the activities. They begin to show some understanding of . . . basic compositional ideas. They talk about differences between their own and others' performance and suggest improvements. They understand how to exercise safely, and describe how their bodies feel during different activities.'

POS Key Stage 1: NC 1a, b, 2a, b, 3a, b, c, 4a, b

Pupils should be taught to:

- Acquire and develop skills.
- Select and apply skills, tactics and compositional ideas.
- Evaluate and improve performance.
- Acquire knowledge and understanding of fitness and health.

Criteria for assessing attainment

- Class working safely: control (including management of apparatus).
- Class answering task: listening, responding, giving feedback.
- Quality produced in response to task.
- Response to teaching.
- Ability to work with others, including apparatus management.
- Improving accuracy and range of movement.
- Increased imaginative/creative performance.
- Ability to do more than one thing at a time.
- Sustained participation.

POS (activity specific): NC 8a, b, c, d

Pupils should be taught to:

- Perform basic skills in travelling, being still, finding space and using it safely, both on the floor and using apparatus.
- Develop the range of their skills and actions.
- Choose and link skills and actions in short movement phrases.
- Create and perform short, linked sequences that show a clear beginning, middle and end and have contrasts in direction, level and speed.

Theme 7: Lifting Body Parts High

Learning about movements and actions where different body parts are above the head

The ability to extend and stretch the body or particular parts of the body is an important feature in gymnastics and has a natural link to work in other areas of the PE curriculum. This theme stimulates the children to think of parts of the body that can be elevated and stretched in different directions while using a variety of points of support (body and that afforded by apparatus). It also encourages them to invert (or reverse the position of) the body while using apparatus and to become more adventurous as skill thresholds rise.

Warm up activities
- Travel in a variety of ways: on feet; hands and feet; large parts of the body.

Floor work
Whole body work
- Find ways of making different parts of the body highest: hands; feet; bottom; tummy; one arm; one foot; knees. Stretch the highest part upwards, towards the ceiling.
- Travel with one part lifted high – change on given signal.
- Develop the above to travel with one part high and then the same part low – change on given signal.

Lower body work
- Jump, lifting parts as high as you can: head; hands; one hand; toes; knees; one toe; heels; chest; back.

Upper body work
- With weight on hands and feet, travel with one part high: bottom; tummy; head; knees; elbows.
- With weight on the hands, lift parts high: bottom; one foot; both feet; knees.

Apparatus work (portable to provide a variety of levels)
- Travel on the apparatus with one part lifted high: head; hands; feet; bottom; one foot; one knee.
- Find places where you can jump *safely* from the apparatus with head high. (Make sure the apparatus is appropriate to the task set. Mats should be provided wherever children are expected to jump from a safe height.)
- Take up a balance position on the apparatus and lift first one part high, then another.
- Find other places on the apparatus to do the same as above.

Cool down activity
- Balance on your back or shoulders. Lift feet as high as possible together and individually. Hold each extension for teacher's count of three.

Lifting body parts high

Theme 8: Feet Together and Apart

Learning about bases of support and body shapes

If previous themes have been covered in depth then this theme will have been reached with the children very much more aware of individual parts of the body, how they can move them in different ways and in different combinations and where all of this can take place. This theme helps them to increase control of their legs particularly, and is a beginning for children to start thinking about clarity and types of body shapes that they can achieve.

Warm up activities
- In your own space, practise and experiment with movements on the floor in which parts of the body are lifted high.
- Practise different ways of travelling that take you to all parts of the hall in a given time span.

Floor work
Whole body work
- Travel on parts of the body with feet together.
- Travel on parts of the body with feet apart.
- In your own space, move on one part of the body to another with: feet apart; feet together. (Are your legs bent or stretched?)

Feet together and apart

Lower body work
- Practise jumping with feet together: on the spot; moving freely about the hall.
- Practise running and jumping: with feet together in the air; with feet apart in the air.
- Find different ways of having the feet together in the air when jumping. Legs can be stretched or bent, in front, behind or to the side of the body.
- Find different ways of having the feet apart in the air when jumping. Legs can be wide or in a scissors position, both bent or stretched, or one bent and one stretched.

Upper body work
- With hands on the floor, practise movements in which your feet are: apart; together.
- Travel in different ways on hands and feet: apart; together.
- Take weight on your hands and lift your feet in the air: one at a time; one after the other; together.
- Take your weight on your hands, jump your feet in the air and bring them down: one after the other; at the same time together; at the same time apart. Concentrate on quiet, controlled landings and always land on your feet.
- Find different ways of making bridges between your hands and your feet: facing the floor; with your back towards the floor; feet apart; feet together.

Apparatus work (portable, linked, and fixed)
- Travel in different ways on the apparatus with: feet together; feet apart.
- Find different ways of hanging from the apparatus with: feet together; feet apart.
- Working on getting your feet above your head, sometimes with feet together and sometimes apart.
- Find different ways of moving from the apparatus to the floor with: feet together; feet apart; legs bent; legs stretched; legs leading; legs following. (Re-emphasise the need for deep controlled landings on two feet when jumping.)

Cool down activity
- Travel with short, quick steps.
- Travel with long, slow steps.

Theme 9: Curling and Stretching

Learning to make different body shapes

Children who have had plenty of experience of taking and transferring weight should be ready to explore the use of the body as it moves between the two extremes of flexion and extension. The ability to extend and flex fully is associated particularly with the spine, and it is from here that movements should begin. Curling can take place by curving the spine forwards, backwards or sideways, while stretching may be achieved by elongating the body or by making it wide. This theme is a very good one in concluding work covered during the Foundation/Key Stage 1 period and also as a lead-in to that to be provided at the beginning of Key Stage 2.

Warm up activities
- Practise any quick movements on the floor, and then ones that are slow and show control.
- Find ways of getting different parts of the body away from the floor from a starting position of choice.

Floor work
Whole body work
- Practise curling the body, taking weight on different body parts.
- Stretch the body, taking weight on different parts. Look to point toes, fingers, stretch the neck.
- In your own space, move with the body curled up.
- In your own space, move with the body stretched out.
- Moving away from your own space, travel changing from curled up shapes to stretched ones, back again, and repeat.

Lower body work
(Note: be aware that young children in this age range will find it very difficult to achieve a tucked shape in the air and then a safe, controlled landing. Jumping to achieve tucked shapes in the air is therefore better left to a later stage when more enhanced performance is possible through practise and consolidation of associated skills.)
- Practise travelling on the feet in a curled/tucked-up position.
- Travel on the feet in a stretched/fully extended position.
- Travel on the feet, sometimes curled/tucked-up and sometimes stretched/fully extended.
- Jump to stretch in the air: wide; long. Work in your own space.

Upper body work
- Travel on hands and feet with the body: curled; stretched.
- With hands on the floor, jump the feet in the air: with legs bent and body curled; with legs and body as stretched as possible, working on keeping the head back in the action.

Apparatus work
Benches and mats
- Practise moving over, on, off and along the bench while: curling the body; stretching the body.
- Display stretched jumps over and off the bench, followed by light landings and curled rolls.

Full apparatus
- Discover places on the apparatus where the body can be: curled; stretched in held positions.
- Travel over the apparatus emphasising: curled movements; stretched movements as you move.
- Link curling and stretching movements, one following the other, as you move across, over, on and off the apparatus.

Links with other themes
- Curl and stretch with *different body parts high*.
- Curl and stretch: *quickly*; *slowly*.

Cool down activity
- Lie on your front or back. Slowly extend to stretch all parts away. On signal slowly draw parts back into the body. Repeat.

Curling and stretching

9 Gymnastics Teaching Material for Years 3 and 4

Themes

1 Use of space
2 Transferring weight
3 Joining movements
4 Directions
5 Parts together and apart

6 Lifting and lowering
7 Shape
8 Speed
9 Twisting and turning

Theme 1: Use of Space

Learning to use space more skilfully

One of the key early themes at the earlier stage was concerned with the need for spacing (and the sharing of space) between individuals working on the floor and on apparatus. This theme now develops a greater awareness of the working space and of where the body can move in relation to the apparatus, as well as the children moving in relation to each other. Later themes are concerned in more detail with space, considering directions, levels and pathways, and the body shape when moving or still in space.

Warm up activities
- Move freely, without stopping, around the floorspace using all the space available. Maintain good awareness of others.
- Travel slowly and quickly, and alternate without stopping.

Floor work
Whole body work
- Travel close to the floor surface on any parts of the body. Maintain lots of contact.
- Travel keeping as little contact with the floor surface as possible.
- Travel in a variety of ways, covering as much floor space physically and generally as possible.
- Travel in a variety of ways in one small area of the floor.

Lower body work
- From a standing position leap in the air to occupy as much air space as possible. Land quietly and with control. Repeat with a two step lead-in.
- Jump to occupy only a small space in the air. Again, land quietly and with control.
- Travel in any way just on the feet, staying in a large free space, as far away from others as possible.
- Walk in a marked, confined space with the rest of the class, but, if possible, without actually touching. Look to reduce space further, then open out.

Upper body work
- With body weight on arms and legs only, try to occupy as much space as possible: facing the floor; with your back towards the floor. Try to hold positions for a count of three.
- With weight equally on arms and legs only, try to occupy a small space. Hold positions achieved for counts of three.
- Taking weight on hands, try to occupy a small space with the feet.
- Travel about the hall taking weight on the hands, and allow the legs to fill as much space as possible. Avoid touching or getting in the way of others.

Apparatus work (portable, linked, and fixed)
- Move freely, using as much of the apparatus as possible.
- Move continuously on and around the apparatus, using only a small section of the apparatus provided.
- Move over, under, around, on, off, up, down or through the apparatus.
- Approach the apparatus from: front; side; back; an angle.
- Leave the apparatus from: front; side; back; an angle.

Cool down activity
- Restrict space (say half the hall, then a quarter or even less). Travel as a group in different directions at half speed, three-quarters, quarter etc. Encourage movement in different directions and in different ways. Avoid touching or getting in the way of others.

A unit of work for Key Stage 2 gymnastics: 'Use of space'

Year: 3	Key Stage: 2	Time (no. of lessons): six sessions (approx. 45 min each)	Title of unit: 'Use of space'	Learning outcome: To develop greater awareness of the working space and where the body can move freely	Cross-curricular elements: Sharing space and collaboration with others; PSHE

Lesson focus on	Lesson 1 General movement	Lesson 2 Lower body work	Lesson 3 Upper body work	Lesson 4 Combining movements	Lesson 5 Practice and improvement	Lesson 6 Performance and assessment
Warm up/introduction	'Ready, steady, go – stop' game. Move freely on signals given. Emphasise use of whole floorspace, looking for space and change of direction.	Repeat game of last week. Provide large coloured cards (red, amber, green) as signals. Emphasise looking, head-up movement, awareness of others, immediate 'stillness' on red.	Repeat closing activity of previous lesson. Vary with movement of different parts (hands and feet combinations, bottoms, backs, fronts, sides etc.).	Warm up travelling about the floorspace taking weight on hands and allowing the legs to fill as much air space as possible (be very aware of others, always returning to floor on feet).	Repeat closing activity of previous lesson. Now take it to another place, following a straight, curved or zigzag pathway. Work on control, with light and springy movements.	Whole-group teacher-led activity. Face teacher in rows, with space between. Making 'wave' actions move towards and away from the teacher. Progress to sideways, diagonals etc.
Floor work	Individual work. Move near to the floor on different body parts. Move away from the floor similarly. Move covering as much or as little floorspace as possible.	Introduce mats. Spread out over the floorspace, making spaces between so that pathways remain. Follow routes provided, avoiding all contact with others. Look to reverse, move sideways, at different speeds etc.	Occupy big spaces by taking weight on arms and legs only. Face the floor, then face the ceiling. Reverse the task to occupy as small a space as possible. Progress to momentary weight only on hands.	Individual work in own space. Practise the above skill. Contrast with making different shapes in the air with the legs (apart, together, one wide and one high, bent knees etc.). Emphasise always returning to feet.	Pairs and threes work. Mark out (with discs, cones, skittles etc.) a mini-area to confine action to. Practise moving towards targets from front, back, side, at an angle, using jumps, rolling and weight-on-hands actions.	Pair up. In your own space show your partner your sequence of actions that 'fill' the floorspace (and the surrounding airspace) a little and a lot. Confine to three different actions that show contrasts.
Apparatus work	Individual choice of mini-apparatus or mat. Confine the above tasks to the area occupied by the equipment. Rotate three times to practise at other equipment.	Introduce benches, box-sections, low surface apparatus (including mats). Travel continuously on the surfaces on the feet, maintaining distance from others. When necessary change direction and pathway followed.	Apply the above tasks to the same apparatus as in the previous lesson (use task cards as a reference point). Pair up and show movements and actions achieved. Work on mirroring your partner's actions.	Full apparatus set-up. Six groups. Move freely using as much or as little of the apparatus as possible. Move over, under, around, on, off, between, up, down or through the apparatus. Group demonstrations.	Full apparatus set-up as in the previous lesson. Rotate groups around at least two different stations. Approach and leave apparatus from front, back, side, an angle, using a full range of movement actions.	Full apparatus set-up as in lessons 4 and 5. Ensure groups are able to use an area not previously visited. Put together an individual sequence that moves towards and away from the apparatus, using a contrast of much and little space used.
Concluding activity	In your own space, make as big a jump in the air as possible to occupy as much space as possible. Repeat with a tucked jump to take up less space in the air. Watch others (half and half demonstration).	Set up a confined space (and further restrict or enlarge as appropriate). Walk the group (or can they jog?) in the confined space without actually touching. Emphasise body movements to achieve the task.	Demonstration by choice. Can actions and movements be improved by slowing them down, performing on different apparatus, greater control? Provide feedback, with markers for the next lesson.	Individually, practise jumps and weight-on-hands combinations. Think about filling large and small spaces on the floor and in the air.	Whole-group demonstrations, all performing at the same time. Emphasise to observers different use of the whole apparatus space and surfaces. Markers for the final session.	Whole-group demonstrations. Record individual performance where applicable. Where does the work progress to next? Extra elements to add: different changes of direction, different pathways followed, changes of speed etc.
Relationships	Individual	Individual	Individual and pairs	Individual and groups	Individual, pairs and groups	Individual, pairs and groups

Resources needed	Attainment Targets: level descriptions 3 and 4	Criteria for assessing attainment
• Mini-apparatus: discs, cones, canes, skittles, skipping ropes, hoops, bean bags etc. • Full range: mats, benches, box sections, nesting tables, climbing frames, movement tables etc. • Task cards, to support apparatus work. • Recording sheets for individuals and, after lesson 4, a large diagram of apparatus set up for reference in lessons 5 and 6. For further development of this theme see 'Use of space' (Years 3 and 4) in the main text.	**Level 3.** 'Pupils select and use skills, actions and ideas appropriately, applying them with coordination and control. They show that they understand tactics and composition by starting to vary how they respond. They can see how their work is similar to and different from others' work, and use this understanding to improve their own performance. They give reasons why warming up before an activity is important, and why physical activity is good for their health.' **Level 4.** 'Pupils link skills, techniques and ideas and apply them accurately and appropriately. Their performance shows precision, control and fluency, and that they understand tactics and composition. They compare and comment on skills, techniques and ideas used in their own and others' work, and use this understanding to improve their performance. They explain and apply basic safety principles in preparing for exercise. They describe what effects exercise has on their bodies, and how important it is to their fitness and health.'	• Class working safely and using space effectively. Increasing skill and control. • Class answering task: listening, responding. • Quality produced in response to task. • Response to teaching. • Ability to work with others. • Accuracy of movement. • Evidence of good design. • Increasingly imaginative performance. • Improvements in sustaining participation.
General physical requirements across all key stages	**POS Key Stage 2: NC 1a, b, 2a, b, 3a, b, 4a, b, c, d**	**POS (activity specific): NC 8a, b, c, d**
• To be physically active, adopt good posture, sustain activity levels. • Continue to develop suppleness, flexibility and muscular strength. • To develop positive attitudes. • To ensure safe practice. • Increasingly to learn to cooperate and work with others.	Pupils should be taught to: • Consolidate their existing skills and gain new ones. • Perform actions and skills with more consistent control and quality. • Plan, use and adapt compositional ideas. • Identify what makes a performance effective. • Understand how exercise affects the body in the short term.	Pupils should be taught to: • Create and perform fluent sequences on the floor and using apparatus. • Include variations in level, speed and direction in their sequence.

Theme 2: Transferring Weight

Learning to acquire greater body control

As a central component of gymnastics is the acquisition of fundamental locomotor skills, learning about control and management of the body when it is moving is an absolute 'must' for young children. The body moves by transferring weight from one part of the body to another or from one part to the same part. Children need lots of opportunities to discover the very great variety of ways in which this can be done with safety and increased competence.

Warm up activities
- Take weight on different parts of the body on one spot. Use lots of or minimal support points; big parts or small parts; combinations of these.
- Practise different ways of travelling on the feet: short sharp steps, long-striding, in different directions, at different speeds etc.

Floor work
Whole body work
- Curl up and practise any rocking movement on your back. Can you rock on your front?
- Practise rocking movements on your front. Can you rock on your side?
- Start in a standing position, and then lower the body to a position where it can rock. Repeat but from a different start position.
- Practise ways of rolling. (Mats could be introduced here to facilitate more comfort to roll execution.)
- Beginning in a standing position, lower the body to the ground, and roll in any direction to bring the feet to a new position for standing.
- Practise your favourite balances.
- With three different ways of balancing, change smoothly from one to the next, holding each position briefly (for a count of three).
- Practise moving continuously, trying to bring as many different parts of the body into contact with the floor as possible.

Lower body work
- Practise ways of taking off and ways of landing with control: one foot to the same foot; one foot to the other foot; two feet to one foot; two feet to two feet. Work on light, controlled and quiet landings.
- Practise deep, light landings, on two feet, with springy rebounds to feet.
- Practise deep, light landings to tucked body, lower weight and roll. (Tuck in head, knees and elbows, allow knees or bottom to touch the ground after the feet, and turn to roll over the back or over one shoulder.)

Upper body work
- With weight on hands and feet, travel over the floor with: front to floor; back to floor; alternately front and back to floor.
- Travel springing from feet to hands, and hands to feet.
- Take weight on your hands, trying to keep the legs up as long as possible. Always bring feet back to the floor quietly, softly and safely.
- Take weight on your hands, lower feet quietly to the floor and: jump and land lightly; lower the body and roll to stand. Repeat and improve this series of actions.

In the early stages of practising handstands, children need to be told to place their hands on the floor with fingers forward (and splayed) and head lifted: 'Look in front of your fingers'. The arms must be straight: 'Like rods of iron'. Legs may be taken up one after the other or together. To avoid overbalancing, the hips may be turned to bring the legs down to one side. A progression for taking weight on hands could be:

1 Crouch jumps.
2 Kicking horses.
3 Handstanding, striving for straight legs and a position of momentary balance (with support from teacher, able fellow pupils, apparatus, wall etc).
4 Balancing on hands.
5 Handstand and lower to crab position.
6 Handstand and lower to forward roll.
7 Cartwheel.

This progression should not necessarily be followed by direct teaching to the whole class, but if plenty of opportunity to work on the hands is given, many will acquire great skill and confidence by the end of the key stage, and move onto attempting handstands with and without support from peers and the teacher.

Apparatus work (portable, linked, and fixed)
- Use the apparatus, moving continuously, trying to bring as many parts of the body into contact with the apparatus surfaces as possible.
- Find places on the apparatus where you can slide. (Inclined benches, planks and ladders are good for this task. Children may also slide along the top of the bar box and movement tables and over the lower rungs of climbing apparatus on to the floor. They need to be told not to slide down ropes, as this can cause the hands to be burned.)
- Travel on the apparatus with large step-like actions of the hands, feet and knees.
- In leaving the apparatus, land lightly and roll in the same direction as the body is travelling. (If landing from a *safe* height, a mat is necessary.)
- Find ways of leaving the apparatus so that body parts other than the feet contact the floor first.

A unit of work for Key Stage 2 gymnastics: 'Transferring weight'

Year: 4	Key Stage: 2	Time (no. of lessons): six sessions (approx. 45 min each)	Title of unit: 'Transferring weight'	Learning outcome: To extend the range of balances for use in personal sequence work	Cross-curricular elements: Continuing to build a movement vocabulary; cooperation; communication; problem-solving skills

	Lesson 1 Large body parts	Lesson 2 Small body parts	Lesson 3 Shape	Lesson 4 Moving into and out of a balance	Lesson 5 Working with partners	Lesson 6 Performance and assessment
Lesson focus on				'Transferring'		
Warm up/introduction	Running and stopping to freeze and hold. Run a few steps, jump and land. Hold balance.	Move about the hall in a variety of ways, on different body parts, and on a signal perform a balance using different parts of the body. Repeat.	Jog around the floorspace and on signal jump up: to tuck jump; to long stretch jump; and to wide star jump.	Move around the floorspace and respond to commands. Left: touch floor with left hand. Right: touch floor with right hand. Jump: show a shape. Etc.	Follow a partner around the floorspace and copy exactly what they do. Repeat but change roles. Emphasise 'balance' movements.	Travel using jumping, rolling, moving on to hands and feet, varying body shapes as movement happens.
Floor work	Explore balancing on a variety of different body parts, e.g. front, back, side, hips. Holding the same base, experiment with changing body shape.	Explore balance on different body parts on the floor. Three-, two- and one-point (large and small) balances. Experiment with different support bases over large and small areas.	Explore stretched and tucked balance shapes around different body parts, e.g. extended, part extended and part contracted around the stomach.	Revise the different parts of the body for balancing. Try different ways of moving into a balance: standing, roll, jump.	Practise one balance so that a partner can jump over. Practise one balance so that a partner can go under without contact.	Make up a sequence with a partner to include a balance, a jump, a roll, movement on hands and on feet. Think about the start and end of the sequence. Perform the sequence.
Apparatus work	Practise balancing on low level apparatus on large body parts. Choose two balances. Repeat them and try to change body shape.	Practise moving on to apparatus and balancing on a variety of small body parts. Choose a balance on a large body part and a small body part and travel between them.	Find different ways of balancing on different parts of the apparatus, holding a stretched, tucked or wide balance based on different body parts and with different points of support from apparatus surfaces.	Travel on to and off apparatus and balance. Travel balance and incorporate mounting and dismounting of apparatus using different parts of the body.	Get on to apparatus from different starting points and arrive on apparatus at the same time. End by leaving at different times. One balances so that the partner can go over or under.	Using the floor and apparatus, work with a partner to produce a sequence. Think about using different body parts, shapes, movement into and out of a balance, moving in a variety of ways.
Concluding activity	Make a sequence of three balances, making sure that they flow from one to the next. Hold each balance for three seconds.	Choose three different balances on different body parts. Practise each balance and 'hold' each for a slow count of three from achieving 'stillness'.	Devise a pattern of three balances showing tucked, stretched and wide shapes, moving between each balance (and 'holding' each for a three-second count).	Perform a roll–balance–roll–balance sequence using two different rolls and balances. Teach your sequence to a partner and try to learn theirs.	Work out a sequence of three balances so that you alternately balance and get over, under and around your partner's balance.	Choose, practise and refine a sequence that you like with a partner. Perform the sequence together to start and end at approximately the same time.
Relationships	Individual	Individual	Individual	Individual and pairs	Pairs	Pairs

Resources needed	Attainment Targets: level descriptions 3 and 4	Criteria for assessing attainment
• Mats, benches, box, ropes, nesting tables, planks. • Class recording sheets. For further development of this theme see 'Transferring weight' in the main text.	**Level 3.** 'Pupils select and use skills, actions and ideas appropriately, applying them with coordination and control. They show that they understand tactics and composition by starting to vary how they respond. They can see how their work is similar to and different from others' work, and use this understanding to improve their own performance. They give reasons why warming up before an activity is important, and why physical activity is good for their health.' **Level 4.** 'Pupils link skills, techniques and ideas and apply them accurately and appropriately. Their performance shows precision, control and fluency, and that they understand tactics and composition. They compare and comment on skills, techniques and ideas used in their own and others' work, and use this understanding to improve their performance. They explain and apply basic safety principles in preparing for exercise. They describe what effects exercise has on their bodies, and how important it is to their fitness and health.'	• Class working safely: control. • Class answering task: listening, responding. • Quality produced in response to task. • Response to teaching. • Ability to work with others. • Accuracy of movement. • Evidence of good design. • Imaginative performance. • Ability to do more than one thing at a time. • Improvements in sustaining participation.
General physical requirements across all key stages	**POS Key Stage 2: NC 1a, b, 2a, b, 3a, b, 4a, b, c, d**	**POS (activity specific): NC 8a, b, c, d**
• To be physically active, adopt good posture. • To maintain flexibility and muscular strength. • To develop positive attitudes. • To ensure safe practice. • Increasingly to learn to cooperate and work with others.	Pupils should be taught to: • Consolidate their existing skills and gain new ones. • Perform actions and skills with more consistent control and quality. • Plan, use and adapt compositional ideas. • Identify what makes a performance effective. • Understand how exercise affects the body in the short term.	Pupils should be taught to: • Create and perform fluent sequences on the floor and using apparatus. • Include variations in level, speed and direction in their sequence.

- Find a variety of ways of travelling on the apparatus in which: the feet are used as much as possible; the hands and feet only are used; the hands grip the apparatus and support the weight in climbing, swinging and hanging; the body supports the weight.

Cool down activity

- In your own space, holding each position for a count of three, show your best small point balance and transfer it to your best large point balance.
- Reverse the above task: large to small.
- Emphasise 'stillness, to movement, to stillness'.

Transferring weight

Theme 3: Joining Movements

Learning to combine body actions

Working progressively towards increasingly improving the smooth and fluent linking of movements is an important feature of gymnastic work. During the earliest stages of work in Key Stage 2 the children should be encouraged to think in terms of continuous movement rather than isolated movements interspersed with periods of rest, wandering and waiting for turns. In order to move continuously, the children must be trained to use the floor as well as the apparatus, to work at a variety of levels and speeds, and in varied directions, working at the same time as their peers. Practice needs to be given in the selection of appropriate ways of linking movements. It also needs to be stressed that thought and planning should precede movement, and that during movement the performer must be alert to the way one action leads naturally into the next. By being required to repeat linked movements, children increase their ability to remember movements and improve the quality and continuity of their work. This is where the beginnings of establishing the notion of the importance of a clear start and a defined finish to movement patterns emerge. The opportunity also exists here to build in the evaluative element to children's work to inform future (improved) performance.

Warm up activity
- Move without stopping, taking weight on many different body parts: on the spot; using all the floor space.

Floor work
Whole body work
- Take weight on one part of the body, hold a stretched position for a count of 3, and then move smoothly to another stretched position on another part of the body – hold for 3 again.
- Practise different ways of rolling. Then join two different ways of rolling together increasing the quality of the link between both rolls.
- Roll slowly and move into another roll in which you move quickly – show good control.
- Rock on a part of the body and then move into a roll before springing lightly to your feet. Repeat and improve the links.
- Show two stretches on different parts, linked by a roll. Repeat and improve.

Lower body work
- Practise varied ways of jumping and landing. Show two different jumps linked together, e.g. one foot to the other and then to two feet; two feet to two feet and then to two feet. Try this around/on a mat, or around a hoop.
- Jump to show a wide stretch and follow it with a jump to show a long stretch. Can you add a tucked jump to this sequence?

- Link ways of travelling on the feet with high jumps in the air and light, controlled landings (vary directions and shapes made in the air).

Upper body work
- Place hands on the floor and jump the feet in the air continuously to show varied shapes and positions of the legs, e.g. both curled, one stretched and one curled, both stretched, legs together, legs wide apart.
- Repeat the above but choose three varied movements and repeat them one after the other. Work on controlled landings throughout.

Combined movements
- Practise jumps and rolls on landing.
- Practise rolling actions and follow them with varied jumps.
- Take weight on hands and roll as the feet touch the floor again.
- Show a stretched jump, land lightly, lower the weight slowly and show a stretched balance on part of the body.
- Make up a sequence including a roll, a balance and a jump. Work on the links between each.

Apparatus work
- Find different ways of getting on the apparatus that allow you to continue moving without a pause.
- Find different ways of leaving the apparatus in which you can continue to move over the floor.
- Move on the apparatus emphasising smooth, continuous movement.
- Select a movement on the apparatus and repeat it three times, thinking particularly about the way in which the movement is linked together.
- Select two different movements on the apparatus and link them together smoothly. Add an extra movement that helps to keep the flow.

Cool down activity
- In your own space practise three times your best two movements joined together. Work particularly on improving start and finish positions.

Joining movements

Theme 4: Directions

Learning about following different pathways

The body has enormous potential in moving in different directions: it can move forwards, backwards, sideways, up or down. Children need to acquire this knowledge and be increasingly aware of the range of possibilities, how a change in direction can be achieved and how apparatus can contribute considerably to building this repertoire of skill. This is a further element to quality aspects of the work and a significant feature of all gymnastic performance.

Warm up activity
- Practise joined movements, e.g. a roll followed by a jump; a balance followed by a roll. Work on improving the links between each movement.

Floor work
Whole body work
- Roll in different directions: forwards; backwards; sideways. Try to link these so that a roll in one direction is followed by another in a different direction.
- Travel on different parts of the body and show a change of direction, sometimes suddenly, sometimes gradually.
- Curl up on the floor and stretch out in different directions, returning to the curled shape each time. Hold the stretch and the start each time for a count of 3.
- From standing, lower the weight backwards, forwards, sideways, to balance on the shoulders. Work to improve the flow of the movement, from the start through to the balance, to the finish.

Lower body work
- Create a pattern of jumps that takes the body in different directions. Look for half, three-quarter, full turns.

Upper body work
- Take the weight on the hands and bring the feet down in different positions. Can you rotate fully with a limited number of moves?

Combined movements
- Jump in the air and roll with a change of direction. Look for a turn made in the air that produces a backward or sideways roll on landing.

Apparatus work (portable, linked, fixed)
- Get on the apparatus in different ways moving forwards and leave the apparatus moving: backwards; sideways.
- Practise getting on the apparatus with a jump: forward; diagonally.
- Travel on the apparatus emphasising varied directions: forwards; backwards; sideways; upwards; downwards.
- Create a sequence, on an area of apparatus of choice, that contrasts at least two directions.

Links with other themes
- Travel *slowly* in one direction *and quickly* in another.
- Travel in one direction with *legs apart* and in another with *legs together*.

Cool down activity
- In open space (on the teacher's command) respond to the call for start, stop, half speed, three-quarter speed, moving forwards, sideways, backwards etc.

Directions

Theme 5: Parts Together and Apart

Learning more about combining actions using different body parts

This theme consolidates and extends some of the work that needs to have gone before on awareness of parts of the body and what can be achieved in a movement sense, and is used here to bring enhanced control and greater variety to the work.

Warm up activity
- Practise a sequence of rolls, jumps and weight-on-hands movements in which the directions change. Look for changes of speed to effect a smooth performance.

Floor work
Whole body work
- With weight on the shoulders, find out which parts of the body can meet and then move far apart, e.g. two feet; foot and knee; knee and shoulder; hands and feet.
- With weight on the tummy, find out which body parts can meet and then move far apart, e.g. feet and hands; feet and head; feet; hands.
- Travel in different ways with feet: near to hands; far away from hands.

Lower body work
- Practise jumping to bring parts near together in the air, e.g. knees to chest, hands and feet, heels to fingers behind the back, heels to back, toe to opposite knee.
- Jump to stretch out as much as possible in the air. Can you make this symmetrical and then asymmetrical? (Both sides the same/different).

Upper body work
- Travel on hands and feet keeping them: close together; far apart. Experiment with different ways.
- Practise balancing on your hands with: feet near to hands; feet stretching as far away from hands as possible.

Apparatus work (portable, linked, fixed)
- Travel in different ways on the apparatus with: hands and feet near to each other; hands and feet far apart.
- Work on finding other parts of the body that can be brought together and then moved far apart on the apparatus, e.g. knees and head, one foot and the opposite hand, heels and the seat, the feet.
- Create a sequence in which you travel with two parts near and then the same two parts far apart. Begin/finish on or off the apparatus.

Cool down activity
- Travel in open space stretching out, away, and into the body, using arms and legs to show this.

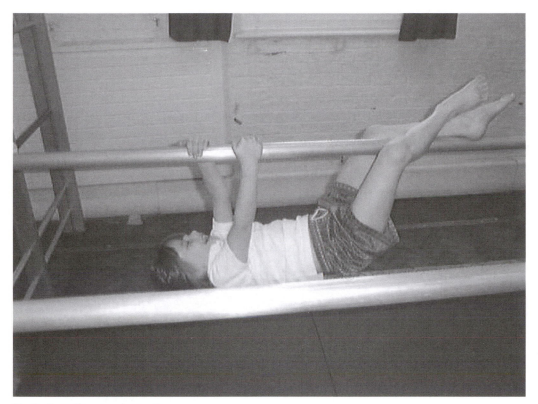

Parts together and apart

Theme 6: Lifting and Lowering

Learning about muscle tension

This theme seeks to emphasise more fully the control needed when different body parts are moved, either against or with gravity. The movements may require strength or demand lightness, qualities that are increasingly coming into play in this age band. This theme gives important practice in the effective use and feeling of 'muscle tension' in movement.

Warm up activity
- Practise a floor sequence in which you are able to show your best movements and greatest control, including smooth transitions between each action performed.

Floor work
Whole body work
- Lift one toe as high as possible when balanced on the following parts of the body: shoulders; tummy; chest; bottom; side. Lower with control.
- From a variety of starting positions lift the following parts of the body high and lower with control: hands; feet; bottom; tummy; one hand and one leg; one leg.
- From a variety of starting positions practise touching the floor as lightly as possible with parts of the body, e.g. bottom from standing, knee from standing on one leg, elbow from standing. Return to a standing position quickly and smoothly.

Lower body work
- Practise leaps or jumps in the air to lift parts of the body as high as possible: hands; knees; head; toes; heels; one leg. The emphasis here is on being able to control the jump and land safely on two feet with a light, springy rebound.

Upper body work
- Practise travelling on hands and feet, and by turning the body, lift bottom and tummy high alternately.
- Practise taking weight on the hands and lift different body parts high, e.g. bottom, heels, one toe, toes. Lower the feet to the floor as slowly and lightly as possible.
- Travel forwards and backwards on one hand, two feet, and stretch the free hand high. Rotate to do the same with other hand.

Combined movements
- Create a sequence of movements in which the legs, arms and body are used to support the weight, and a variety of parts are lifted high.

Apparatus work (portable, linked, fixed)
- Find different ways of using apparatus surfaces to lift different parts of the body high, and then use the same part(s) to help support the weight in a balance.
- Travel on the apparatus in which different parts of the body are high, e.g. head, one leg, hands, both legs, bottom.
- Use the apparatus in different ways to lift first the feet high and then the arms or head.
- Find different ways of lifting the body, or parts of the body, in which a degree of strength is required.
- Find ways of lowering the body or parts of the body as slowly and lightly as possible, on to other apparatus surfaces, and back to the floor.

Cool down activity
- Practise lowering and lifting from front body (press-up) position on hands and feet only. Keep control over the movement – no 'collapsing'.
- Invert the practice (turn the other way so that children are facing the ceiling).

Lifting and lowering

Theme 7: Shape

Learning more about the variety of shapes the body can make

An important element of efficient motor function is body image, and to help to develop this children need to be encouraged to develop an awareness of the outline of the body, both when holding a still position and when they are moving. The four basic shapes are wide, long, curled and twisted, but these will be modified considerably by the way in which the body is supported or suspended, and the need to adapt the shape to the spaces and different surfaces presented by a range of apparatus. When working on this theme, clarity of body shape in still positions should be explored before shape in movement can be appreciated. There is a danger, therefore, that the work will become static, and this needs to be guarded against by encouraging linking movements and actions of a dynamic nature. In the appreciation of body shape, observation of others is an important feature that needs to be integrated into the learning experience. The theme also makes an important contribution to adopting good body posture, a vital cog in fluent and efficient motor performance.

Warm up activities
- Practise a sequence of: three jumps; three balances; or three ways of taking weight on hands.
- Sit and watch a partner's sequence, and then show your sequence to him or her.
- Comment on each other's performance, with an emphasis on the shapes achieved.

Floor work
Whole body work
- Supporting the weight on different parts, make the body: as wide as possible; as curled up as possible; as long and stretched as possible; as twisted as possible. (For the twisted shape, part of the body should be kept in contact with the floor and the rest of the body and limbs rotated around that part. Think about 'rotating around a fixed pin'.)
- By supporting weight in one way (e.g. on hands and feet only or on the bottom), show each of the four shapes in turn.
- Move low over the floor with the body: curled; stretched wide; stretched long.
- Repeat the above task but with the body away from the floor at a medium, then a high, level.

Lower body work
- Practise jumping to show different body shapes in the air. (Care needs to be taken in the curled position to open for a light, resilient, springy landing. The twisted shape can be shown by looking over one shoulder at raised heels, or down at the floor to the side, or through the legs.)

Upper body work
- Practise taking weight on hands to show varied shapes with the legs.
- Try to balance on the hands and show two shapes with the legs before bringing the feet lightly to the ground, e.g. together and stretched, and wide and stretched.
- Try to show a shape with the legs while moving from feet to hands to feet, repeating this sequence.

Combined movements
- Show varied shapes when rolling, jumping, balancing and taking weight on hands, e.g. a wide stretched jump, followed by a curled roll and a long narrow balance on the shoulders.

Apparatus work (portable, linked, fixed)
- Show varied body shapes on the apparatus when jumping, climbing, hanging, circling, heaving, taking weight on hands or in a position of balance.
- Emphasise one particular body shape on the apparatus: wide; long; curled; twisted.
- Find places where body shapes can be held, and link them together with quick movements. Work on maintaining the shape held for a count of three.

Cool down activity
- Show one body shape in particular on the floor: wide; long; curled; twisted. Look to extend and/or contract all parts of the body depending on the shape performed.

Shape

Theme 8: Speed

Learning about applying changes of speed to movement

The theme of 'speed', like 'directions' and 'shape', adds qualitative elements to gymnastics work. In all aspects of movement an element of time is involved. Some actions require quick, immediate speed for their efficient performance, while others can best be carried out in a slow, deliberate manner. Children can best learn the effect of varied speeds on movements by exploring at first the extremes of quick and slow. Later they may experience the sensation of accelerating and decelerating as they perform gymnastic movements.

Warm up activities
- Practise your favourite movements on the floor from the last lesson.
- Find how many different ways you can balance the body on hands and feet only.

Floor work
Whole body work
- Practise rolling as slowly as possible.
- Practise rolling as quickly as possible. (Mats need to be provided as control is likely to be lost in the children's natural desire to work quickly.)
- Plan a sequence of different shapes taking the weight on parts of the body. Perform the sequence: slowly; as quickly as possible. Try to have a mix – some shapes moving slowly, others quickly.

Lower body work
- Travel on the feet with very short, quick movements.
- Travel by lifting one leg at a time slowly and as high as possible.
- Plan a sequence of 3 jumps on the spot and repeat them quickly, one following the other as soon as possible after landing from the previous.

Upper body work
- Until the children have developed and refined the skill of managing taking weight on their hands, the range of speed at which they can work will be limited. The more able may be able to vary the speed with which the legs move up from the ground and the speed of performing cartwheels, and may lower legs from handstanding quickly, or slowly, but always working with control, returning the feet to floor first.

Apparatus work
Benches and mats
- Practise moving over, along, round, on, off, from side to side: slowly; quickly.
- Practise moving along and away from the bench quickly, and then work at a very slow speed on the floor.

Full apparatus
- Practise using the apparatus as slowly as possible, but maintain continuous movement.
- (Half the class working, half watching.) Repeat the same movements as quickly as possible – emphasise working safely and under control.
- Experiment with different movements on the apparatus and find whether they are best performed slowly or quickly. Which ones are more easily controlled?
- Choose one quick movement and one slow movement, and link them together in a sequence. Reverse so that the slow movement comes first.
- Choose a simple movement that can be repeated. Perform it several times: with an increase in speed; starting quickly and decreasing speed.
- Perform a sequence that comes to a climax by having a quick movement at the end.
- Perform a sequence that has a slow, controlled finish.

Cool down activity
- Perform a movement in free space that you can continuously do *slowly*.

Theme 9: Twisting and Turning

Learning to increase the number of linking actions

Twisting and turning are body actions that require some definition and clarity of explanation. A twist occurs when one part of the body is fixed and the rest of the body is rotated to produce torsion (twisting). In a turn, the whole body rotates about an axis, as in jumping to face a new direction, forward or backward rolling, or cartwheeling. Twisting and turning are both important body actions in gymnastics, in that both can be used to link movements and to establish new directions in which to continue travelling during sequences. Twisting and turning also represent additional qualitative elements of overall gymnastic performance.

Warm up activities
- Create your own opening activity in which you get warm, stretch the body and practise a particular gymnastic skill that you feel you do well.

Floor work
Whole body work
- Practise turning the body by rolling forwards, backwards and sideways.
- Fix a part of the body on the floor (e.g. shoulders, knees and one hand, hands and one leg) and practise twisting the body around that fixed part.
- Balance on the floor and twist to bring a new part to support the body. Continue this practice repetitively so that the twisting action always takes you to a new balance position.

Lower body work
- Practise turning the body by rotating in the air. How far can you turn: halfway, three-quarters, the whole way?
- Practise twisting the body in the air by turning the arms and legs in opposite directions.
- Practise taking off from one foot and use your free leg to help you turn. Try the same from the opposite foot.

Upper body work
- Take weight on hands and bring your feet down in a new place by twisting the hips. Can you move through 90 degrees?
- Practise trying to turn the body over from feet to hands to feet (the beginnings of cartwheeling).

Apparatus work (portable, linked, fixed)
- Find places where part of the body can be fixed, and twist the rest of the body.
- Travel on the apparatus by turning the body, e.g. rotating around a pole, beam or two ropes; turning to face new directions on the climbing frame, ropes and table or box tops.
- Find ways of getting on and off the apparatus to show a change of direction – achieve this by using a twist or a turn.
- Find ways of supporting the body and twist to a new support.

Links with other themes
- Change from *curling* to *stretching* and then from *stretching* to *curling* with a twist.
- Have *body parts near or far apart*, changing from one to the other with a twist.

Cool down activity
- Find ways of travelling continuously (at a slow pace) throughout the whole space: rotating, twisting, turning, near to/away from the floor and extending/contracting the body as you go.

Twisting and turning

10 Gymnastics Teaching Material for Years 5 and 6

Themes

1 Sequences
2 Levels
3 Partner work
4 Flight
5 Pathways

6 Symmetry and asymmetry
7 Balance and continuity
8 Flow
9 Strength and lightness

Theme 1: Sequences

Learning to develop more complex series of actions

A theme visited earlier was concerned with the joining of movements. The ability to show continuity and flow of movement in transferring weight is a vitally important feature of gymnastic work. Earlier work encouraged children to think about their movements in readiness to experiment and practise their responses to particular tasks set. Now, as children become increasingly more versatile, thought and action need to be more intrinsically linked to produce more complete movement sequences. Sequences will often be demanded that are appropriate to particular tasks set by the teacher. These sequences should have a definite starting position, illustrate the theme in continuous action, show varied and original work and have a clear and controlled finishing position – elements of gymnastic work expected of children as they near the end of the primary age phase.

Warm up activities

- Warm up by practising movements that are vigorous (jumps, leaps, weight on hands) and balances that stretch the body. Work out your own patterns of movement, so that there is a link between each action performed.

Floor work

Whole body work
- Practise standing, rolling and standing repetitively.
- Walk, roll and continue walking. Continue to repeat the pattern.
- Stand, stretch, lower the body, stretch on another part, bring feet to floor and stand. (Emphasise particularly the transition from one position to another.) Repeat and improve the pattern.

Lower body work
- Travel with high leaps from foot to foot (take off on one foot, stretch the other to land on the same leading leg).
- Link jumps together with running movements. Vary the speed to maintain control, particularly for landings.
- Plan a sequence of jumping, running and leaping movements that are thought out beforehand. Practise, modify, improve, perform.

Sequences

Upper body work
- Travel using hands and feet alternately. Progress competence in cartwheeling actions – emphasise lightness when feet land and contact the floor.

Combined movements

Emphasise the importance of starting and finishing all sequences in a clear, controlled position of stillness.

- Roll and jump to stretch. Vary the directions and speeds of the roll.
- Roll and take weight on the hands, momentarily and for increasing periods of time.
- Create a sequence that includes a jump, a roll, a balance and a movement in which the weight is on the hands – the actions can be performed in any order.
- Create a floor sequence in which there is: a change of direction; a change of speed – make these very clear.

Apparatus work (portable, linked, fixed)

- Begin a sequence of actions on the floor, move continuously on the apparatus and move back to the floor. Repeat this sequence, improving the links between the movements.
- Find a movement on the apparatus that can be repeated in a rhythmic way, e.g. circling or swinging on a bar or beam. Add a definite starting and a finishing position.
- Create a sequence in which there is: a change of speed; a change of direction, using a mixture of floor area and apparatus surfaces.
- Practise linking one piece of apparatus with another in a sequence that includes using the floor.

Cool down activity

- Continue sequence work by practising and repeating your favourite floor sequence.

A unit of work for Key Stage 2 gymnastics: 'Sequences'

Year: 6	Key Stage: 2	Time (no. of lessons): six sessions (approx. 45 min each)	Title of unit: 'Sequences'	Learning outcome: To show increased continuity in performing organised series of movement action	Cross-curricular elements: Consolidation of 'sequence' understanding; PSHE elements

	Lesson 1 Linking core actions	Lesson 2 Improving timing and cooperation	Lesson 3 Complexity of movement	Lesson 4 Coordinating movement to music	Lesson 5 Modification and improvement	Lesson 6 Performance and potential
Lesson focus on						
Warm up/introduction	'Free the statues' game. When tagged by one of three red-bibbed runners make a statue with a defined shape. Two green-bibbed runners free the statue. Rotate reds and greens. Emphasise looking for space and evasion, but also clear and very still body shapes when caught.	'Follow my leader' game. Using the whole floorspace, copy (by following the same route) your partner's actions and movements.	Working individually in free space, improve links between actions. Make the end of one movement flow into the beginning of the next. What actions are best for this?	To a musical background perform actions (jumps, rolls, balances etc.) to suit. Work on flow and continuity of movement to match rhythm and beat.	Different music (upbeat). Teacher-led warm up exercises.	In groups, own choice of whole-body warm up exercises.
Floor work	Individual work. Link balances, rolls, jumps in preferred order. Improve links between each action. Have clear start and finish positions.	Stay with your partner to practise symmetrical and asymmetrical actions. Practise jumps, balances, rolls etc.	In groups of three and four work on increasing the number of movements in sequences. Contrast levels, speed, direction, shape etc.	Group apparatus set up. Practise, refine and perform final group sequences. Perform as individual groups for others to observe and to be filmed. Invite feedback.	In groups, revise favourite routines (encourage variety, similarity, creativity, cooperation etc.). Practise basic actions in open space.	Practise the core actions of individual sequences in own free floorspace. Refine qualitative elements, particularly flow and continuity, links and response to chosen group music.
Apparatus work	Four large apparatus areas. Repeat the above task on apparatus surfaces and surrounding floor area. Experiment with different starting and finishing points and with the levels worked at.	Set up apparatus areas as in the previous lesson. In a different area work in threes and fours as in the last lesson to devise sequences that show symmetrical and asymmetrical actions and movements on a variety of surfaces.	Apply the above task to apparatus. Film some samples for feedback at the end of the lesson (or in the classroom later) and identify areas to work on next week.	Own choice of apparatus, restricted to three pieces (linked or separate). Construct with sequences and the music in mind. Practise, refine and when ready demonstrate.	Apparatus set up as groups choose. Apply work to apparatus surfaces and floor surrounds with their own of the teacher's music of choice. Teacher films progress for later feedback.	Groups set up apparatus. Groups practise, revise, practise and perform finalised sequences. These are filmed and comment from others observing is invited.

Concluding activity	Work with a partner. Combine your sequences, mirror or match, or perform at the same time in a defined area on and around the apparatus. Select a pair to demonstrate from each area. Invite comment and feedback to inform next week's work.	Perform sequences in groups. Invite commentary and feedback. Alert the future video pupils to the recording of their efforts.	Individual choice of warm down activity. Suggest stretches and/or bending activities that are controlled, fluent and performed very quietly.	Video for feedback purposes and for further development in the next lesson. Do any children want to bring their own music. Repeat last session's choice of warm down activity.	Discuss modifications to routines needed before final lesson. Warm down led by the teacher focusing on controlled stretches and bending exercises around the body axis.	Discuss potential for a class assembly. Where does the work progress to next? Is there potential for a larger group performance, or for highlighting individual or paired work within the whole? Other themes to visit: flight, continuity, flow, strength, lightness etc.
Relationships	Individual, groups and pairs	Pairs, threes and fours	Individual and groups	Individual and groups	Individual and groups	Groups

Resources needed

- Full range: mats, benches, box, ropes, nesting tables, movement tables, linking planks etc.
- Class recording sheets.

For further development of this theme see 'Sequences' in the main text.

General physical requirements across all key stages

- To be physically active, adopt good posture, sustain activity levels.
- Maintain and develop flexibility and muscular strength.
- To develop positive attitudes.
- To ensure safe practice.
- Increasingly to learn to cooperate and work with others.

Criteria for assessing attainment

- Class working safely: control.
- Class answering task: listening, responding.
- Quality produced in response to task.
- Response to teaching.
- Ability to work with others.
- Accuracy of movement.
- Evidence of good design.
- Increasingly imaginative performance.
- Ability to do increasingly more complex linked actions.
- Sustained participation.
- Greater use of all gymnastic elements (speed, direction, flow, control etc.).

Attainment Targets: level descriptions 3 and 4

Level 3. 'Pupils select and use skills, actions and ideas appropriately, applying them with coordination and control. They show that they understand tactics and composition by starting to vary how they respond. They can see how their work is similar to and different from others' work, and use this understanding to improve their own performance. They give reasons why warming up before an activity is important, and why physical activity is good for their health.'

Level 4. 'Pupils link skills, techniques and ideas and apply them accurately and appropriately. Their performance shows precision, control and fluency, and that they understand tactics and composition. They compare and comment on skills, techniques and ideas used in their own and others' work, and use this understanding to improve their performance. They explain and apply basic safety principles in preparing for exercise. They describe what effects exercise has on their bodies, and how important it is to their fitness and health.'

POS Key Stage 2: NC 1a, b, 2a, b, 3a, b, 4a, b, c, d

Pupils should be taught to:

- Consolidate their existing skills and gain new ones.
- Perform actions and skills with more consistent control and quality.
- Plan, use and adapt compositional ideas.
- Identify what makes a performance effective.
- Understand how exercise affects the body in the short term.

POS (activity specific): NC 8a, b, c, d

Pupils should be taught to:

- Create and perform fluent sequences on the floor and using apparatus.
- Include variations in level, speed and direction in their sequence.

Theme 2: Levels

Learning to build skill performance around different levels and heights

When using the floorspace the body may move at a low level or with parts reaching to a high level. A jump is a good example of an action that can be used to take the body higher still in relation to the floor. This use of levels brings interest and variety to floor work. Similarly, on the apparatus the body may work at varied levels, near the point of support or stretching away both above and below it, and also possibly away from it. Apparatus will provide opportunities to move from one level to another, from floor to apparatus and vice versa.

Warm up activities
- Create a floor sequence that has a clear beginning and end. Perform it twice, making it as much alike as possible on each occasion.
- Observe a partner and comment. Highlight one specific aspect of the sequence that could be improved.

Floor work
Whole body work
- Practise balancing the body on a small body part: keeping as near the floor as possible; then stretching high.
- Find different and varied ways of travelling on parts of the body: keeping near to the floor; then with parts reaching high.

Lower body work
- Travel on the feet in a low position. Gradually get higher and finish with a jump.
- Reverse the above. Start with a jump, land and gradually get lower to finish with a travelling action, body close to the floor and a concluding balance achieving 'stillness'.

Upper body work
- Practise springing on to the hands and finish with the body low.
- Repeat the above, springing on to the hands, but now trying to lift the legs high into the air.

Apparatus work (portable, linked, fixed)
- Practise travelling on the apparatus at: a low level; a high level.
- Travel on the apparatus so that: you go from low to high; you go from high to low. (Safety aspects and control are important here. Mats must be provided if the movement down from a height involves jumping.)
- Travel on the apparatus so that the body is kept near to the point of support.
- Travel on the apparatus so that the body stretches away from the point of support: above; below.

- Make a sequence that shows a contrast of levels, in relation to both the height at which you are working and the point of support.

Cool down activity
- Combine one movement near the floor and one away from the floor (in either order) which emphasises work performed at different levels.

Theme 3: Partner Work

Learning to work with a partner to produce combined action sequences

The 'educational' approach to teaching primary school gymnastics promoted throughout these materials does not require children to assist and support each other to perform vaults or agilities. However, to work with a partner in order to create movement sequences on both floor and apparatus can be a rewarding experience for all concerned, and that includes the teacher. The children are challenged both physically and socially to cooperate in answering movement tasks set by the teacher, and given scope for creating and performing their own ideas.

It would be unwise to start on partner work with a class that has not already achieved a good standard of individual work. The children should be experienced in managing their bodies on apparatus and in working to interpret themes in a creative and imaginative way, and able to work sensibly as individuals in a group situation. With a new class, or one that has not yet reached a stage of responsible self-discipline, it is better not to try partner work until the children have shown that they are ready to accept the difficult challenge of adapting their movements to another person. An experienced and skilful class can go on to develop work in which threes and fours cooperate to produce patterns of movement, but the more children there are in a group the more the quality of the finished sequence will be affected by individual variations in performance.

In introducing children to partner work, the following points should be considered by the teacher:

1 A good standard of individual work should already have been achieved.
2 Children are best left to choose their own partners, except when it may be necessary to match up particular body types, or for reasons of 'desirable or less desirable' pairings.
3 The tasks set and the arrangement of apparatus used should not be overcomplicated or too complex initially.
4 Time needs to be allowed for discussion, experimentation, practice and observation. It can often appear that a class working on partner work is noisy and unproductive. This is a natural stage as ideas are being worked out, and decisions made, which in turn may need modification and further practice. This process all takes time if the ultimate aim is to produce good quality work that has been planned through a shared experience.
5 Children should be encouraged to select and clarify their movements together. A short sequence of controlled movement which answers the task set is always preferable to a long series of movements that peter out because they are over-complicated and too complex.

6 Partner (or group) sequences should eventually be performable with little significant change or difference when the children are required to repeat the actions and movements, for the benefit of others to appreciate.

7 Once a class is skilled in partner work, it can become a key feature of subsequent lessons. In addition to the tasks and ideas suggested in this section, most other themes can be interpreted by children cooperating in twos, threes or fours. Beyond this, potentially bigger groupings are possible when the experience is well established as a part of gymnastics provision.

Partner tasks

Following

- One partner links a series of gymnastic movements together, either on the floor or on apparatus, and the other follows the same pathway, repeating the movements. The sequence initially should be short and clearly defined. The leader should show the sequence at least twice before an attempt is made to work together. More complex tasks can be set as experience and competence develop.

Matching and Mirroring

- Partners perform the same movements, either one after the other or at the same time. They might move facing each other as in a mirror, be side by side or move one behind the other. The pathways followed may be parallel, coming together and moving away or one following the pathway set by the leader. Remember it is not easy for children to copy each other's movements exactly. There is always the problem of a variation in ability to perform particular movements, and of differences in timing. Each child will need to adapt and change movements to fit in with their partner.
- The teacher should encourage *both* children to take the initiative in leading and suggesting movements. The finished sequence will then be a joint effort that should have involved fully both partners. Learning to adapt to each child's ability is a crucial learning experience to emphasise here.

Contrasting

- Each of the partners works to show differences of timing, shape, actions, levels or directions in their movements. Suitable tasks would be: moving and stopping; quick and slow; parts high, parts low; parts together, parts apart; curling and stretching; levels, high and low; directions, upwards and downwards; shape, rounded and long, stretched or tucked.
- Contrast is best demonstrated by showing the extremes of movement. One partner may confine movements to one extreme while the other shows the contrasting quality. Or it may be that *each* will show the extremes of movement, either one after the other or at the same time.

Partner work

Passing over, under, around
- When beginning this task, movements need to be neither matched nor contrasted. One partner can operate as an obstacle that the other will negotiate by passing over, under or around without touching. One may remain as the obstacle throughout the sequence, or roles may change once or several times during the sequence. Normally the obstacle will remain still when being negotiated. For classes who have worked for some time on this task, it might be suggested that partners should match or contrast their movements. For example, one partner might make a rounded shape on the floor while the other moves over, showing a contrasting wide, stretched shape in the air. Introducing different apparatus will lend further opportunities to this aspect of the work.

Supporting
- Children are involved by being in physical contact and assisting each other: to maintain a balance; to take all or part of one partner's weight; to travel; to help one partner to gain flight. This work in which one person takes some responsibility for another's work is suitable only for an advanced and more skilful class. Plenty of time needs to be allowed to explore possibilities on the floor using mats only, before adding the extra difficulties posed by extra apparatus. When apparatus is introduced it should not be overcomplex, and the teacher should give careful directions about its use. Benches are suitable for balancing tasks and assisting

flight. Two or three pairs may be allocated to each bench according to the number available and the size of the class. Alternatively, half the class may work using benches, while the others use mats. The beginnings of 'spotting' skills can be reasonably broached here, with simple guidance given on helping partners to re-establish balance. The teacher role in assisting all of this is a crucial element in assuring safety in the work and potentially quality outcomes.

Work in threes and fours
- Suitable tasks for working in small groups may be developed from the ideas suggested from the previous partner work. Moving together and then apart with matched movements, following common pathways, two working as a pair to contrast with movements of a third, one assisting two to maintain a balance or two assisting one to achieve flight are all possible challenges for an experienced class. There is great potential here to challenge the children to produce very interesting and creative gymnastic work through a team approach to planning.

Cool down activity
- Pair or group up and copy/match a series of stretches to limber down (individual children or the teacher could lead this).

Partner work

Theme 4: Flight

Learning to move skilfully in the air

This theme is concerned with the movement of the body through the air, how this is achieved and how to establish a sense of increasing control throughout, including, crucially, landings. The teacher's focus here is on the different ways of propelling the body into the air, control and movements of the body during flight and the achievement of safe, resilient and ever increasingly light landings. Flight will have been a feature of most lessons from the earliest stages. Children should already have developed a confidence about taking off and landing, but the idea of increasing the time spent in the air will be relatively new to them. The skill and confidence necessary to advance skill in flight needs to be built up slowly, with care, and with control as the overriding feature of the work.

Warm up activities
- Work with a partner to show a sequence of 4 actions in which you match your movements.
- Help and support your partner to balance on small parts of the body.

Floor work
Lower body work
- Practise different take-offs and landings: from one foot to the same foot; from one foot to the opposite foot; from one foot to two feet; from two feet to one foot; from two feet to two feet. Which is the one you do best, with most control?
- Take off to show different body shapes in the air: wide and stretched; long and stretched; curled; twisted. Can you work on showing a more defined (longer held shape) shape in the air? How is this achieved?
- Practise jumping for: height; distance. (Emphasise the importance of maintaining control and resilience in landing.)
- Practise jumping to turn in the air. What shapes are possible in this movement?

Upper body work
- Practise moving from hands to feet and back again in varied ways, e.g. move from one foot to hands and then to two feet. (Hands and arms should develop the same resilience encouraged in receiving weight on the feet and legs. Think about the 'springiness' required to do this well.)
- From a jump to land on feet, take the weight on the hands and arms and: curl to roll forwards; push back on to feet. Repeat and try to emphasise the springing actions in this task.

Apparatus work (portable, linked, fixed)
- Find ways of jumping down safely from a height, benches, inclined planks, bar-box, trestle. (Keep the head up in flight. Use mats for landing.)

- Find ways of getting on to the apparatus with a jump or leap and immediately jump off, returning to the floor.
- Find ways to move from apparatus surface to surface (where layout provides such opportunities), with jumps and landings that maintain control throughout.
- Find ways of coming off the apparatus (back to the floor), taking weight carefully on the hands and then sweeping the legs as high as possible.
- Use ropes, rings or trapeze to assist the body to swing through the air. (Dismount on the back swing, returning to the floor.)
- Use beams, poles and ropes to allow the body to hang from the hands. Swing the body and release to land, on the floor, safely and with control.
- Show flight to achieve different body shapes in the air. (Encourage jumping *up* rather than down when moving from apparatus to the floor. For this reason the apparatus for flight situations need not be too high.)
- Show flight in jumping from apparatus to land and adopt a balance on varied body parts – reiterate the need to jump up initially to 'show' the flight element.

Cool down activity
- Practise three times your best take-off, jump and landing either to land back from take-off point or to land (under control) behind, in front or to the side.

A unit of work for Key Stage 2 gymnastics: 'Flight'

Year: 5	Key Stage: 2	Time (no. of lessons): six sessions (approx. 45 min each)	Title of unit: 'Flight'	Learning outcome: To develop a greater sense of movement 'in the air', from take-off, through flight, to landing	Cross-curricular elements: Increasing support for each other through collaborative tasks; PSHE elements

	Lesson 1 Revise jumping skills	Lesson 2 Combined movements	Lesson 3 Improving resilience	Lesson 4 Assisted flight	Lesson 5 Practice and improvement	Lesson 6 Performance and assessment
Warm up/introduction	Revise individual jumping skills. Bent knees for take-off and landing. Practise for height and distance. Work on using the arms to assist upward leverage.	Practise individual jumping skills. Work on control, spring in take-off and resilience in landing. What shapes and turns are possible in the 'flight phase'?	In own choice of space, practise *big* springy jumps and light, resilient landings. Re-emphasise bent knees for take-off and landing. Build in a controlled start and finish.	Scatter hoops around the floorspace. Warm up individually, targeting hoops to jump into and out of. Look for a depth of jump that allows for a controlled and balanced landing.	Jump for height on the spot. Travel around the floorspace and on signal link to jump for height. Practise jumping for distance but with a controlled landing. Emphasise 'depth of jump' to facilitate this.	Make up your own pathway (circular, square, zigzag, curved etc.) of jumps to follow, with clear pauses (about two seconds) before the next take-off. Work on control, shapes in the air, quality landings.
Floor work	Individual work. Take-offs and landings (one foot, two feet, from one to another, from two to one, from one to the same foot etc.). Work on keeping the head up.	Practise moving from feet to hands and back to feet repetitively. Add variety to this (from one foot to both hands, from both feet to one hand etc.).	Practise a variety of different jumps, with different shapes in the flight phase, leading to landings that are balanced on different body parts. Sample some efforts illustrating key elements.	Introduce mats (for four groups). Extend run-up to land on mat (ideally near the centre). Introduce the idea of 'spotters', positioned at the sides, to help the jumper to regain balance.	In pairs (use mats if desired). Teach the leap-frog from a standing position, to flight phase, to landing. Emphasise head up looking forwards throughout. Work on erasing recoil on landing.	Mats shared by pairs. Using jumping skills travel on, around, off surface for periods of 10 seconds. Then tag partner to continue. Work on keeping the head up, springiness etc.
Apparatus work	Low level apparatus (locate all round the floorspace). Target landings on to mats. Work on controlled landings, re-establishing balance. Work on showing a variety of body shapes in the air.	Low level apparatus (as previous lesson). Apply the above tasks to the surfaces provided. Build the beginnings of a sequence that includes weight-on-hands action, rolls linked by high, springy jumps.	Add some higher surfaces (e.g. higher nesting tables, inclined planks, benches, higher box, movement tables). Jump to dismount at points that are *safe*, landing on mats and with the head kept up in flight.	Add springboards (or other surfaces to spring off). Repeat practice above with greater emphasis on using the assisted flight achieved to show a more defined shape in the air. Continue with spotters.	Full apparatus set up and now linked to enable a sequence that shows 'pauses' in the action before exit from the apparatus. Jump on, perform an action of choice (roll, balance, another jump etc.) on the apparatus, then jump off.	Full apparatus set up as in previous lesson. Choose an apparatus area to put together a series of actions that highlight jumping skills. Restrict to about a 10-second time frame. Repeat and improve ready for performance.
Concluding activity	In own space. Quarter, half and three-quarter turns in the air in free space. Attempt a full turn. Emphasise key principles of jumping and landing skills.	Half the class show and half observe performance of the above tasks. Invite commentary and feedback. Emphasise markers for the next lesson. Warm down stretch of choice.	Find ways of mounting apparatus with a jump that is immediately followed with a jump off. Sample efforts and emphasise control and resilience elements.	Group by group, demonstrate the variety of take-offs (one-footed and two-footed) and shapes and landings performed. Emphasise control throughout, from start to finish.	Group demonstrations. Look for variety and different interpretations of the previous task. Markers for final lesson highlighted.	Whole-group demonstrations. Record individual performance where applicable. Where does the work progress to next? Extra elements to add: different changes of direction, different pathways followed, changes of speed etc.
Relationships	Individual	Individual	Individual	Individual and groups	Individual, pairs and groups	Individual, pairs and groups

Resources needed	Attainment Targets: level descriptions 3 and 4	Criteria for assessing attainment
- Full range: mats, benches, box, springboards, nesting tables, climbing frames, movement tables, linking planks etc. - Task cards, to support apparatus work. - Class recording sheets. For further development of this theme see 'Flight' in the main text.	**Level 3.** 'Pupils select and use skills, actions and ideas appropriately, applying them with coordination and control. They show that they understand tactics and composition by starting to vary how they respond. They can see how their work is similar to and different from others' work, and use this understanding to improve their own performance. They give reasons why warming up before an activity is important, and why physical activity is good for their health.' **Level 4.** 'Pupils link skills, techniques and ideas and apply them accurately and appropriately. Their performance shows precision, control and fluency, and that they understand tactics and composition. They compare and comment on skills, techniques and ideas used in their own and others' work, and use this understanding to improve their performance. They explain and apply basic safety principles in preparing for exercise. They describe what effects exercise has on their bodies, and how important it is to their fitness and health.'	- Class working safely and using space effectively. Increasing skill and control. - Class answering task: listening, responding. - Quality produced in response to task. - Response to teaching. - Ability to work with others and the beginnings of 'spotting' skills. - Accuracy of movement. - Evidence of good design. - Increasingly imaginative performance. - Improvements in sustaining participation. - Understanding of 'flight' as a movement theme.
General physical requirements across all key stages	**POS Key Stage 2: NC 1a, b, 2a, b, 3a, b, 4a, b, c, d** Pupils should be taught to:	**POS (activity specific): NC 8a, b, c, d** Pupils should be taught to:
- To be physically active, adopt good posture, sustain activity levels. - Continue to maintain and develop suppleness, flexibility and muscular strength. - To develop positive attitudes. - To ensure safe practice. - Increasingly to learn to cooperate and work with others.	- Consolidate their existing skills and gain new ones. - Perform actions and skills with more consistent control and quality. - Plan, use and adapt compositional ideas. - Identify what makes a performance effective. - Understand how exercise affects the body in the short term.	- Create and perform fluent sequences on the floor and using apparatus. - Include variations in level, speed and direction in their sequence.

Theme 5: Pathways

Learning to increase the routes taken in preparing gymnastic actions

A pathway describes the path of the body or part of the body through space. Pathways can be straight, curved or twisted, as well as tracing particular patterns on the floor (and potentially on different apparatus surfaces), e.g. circles, squares, zig-zags. Encouraging children to use a range of different pathways, rather than only the most obvious, adds much variety to their eventual work, and is also useful in helping groups to share restricted floor space and apparatus. As a much visited aspect of work from the early practices of learning to run and dodge, and learning how to use all parts of the workspace independently of each other, in the later years of the primary age phase this theme is important and will make a telling contribution to especially qualitative elements of the work produced. It is revisited here to bring a greater variety of floor pattern to sequences, and to consider possible pathways in space when moving on, off, over and along a variety of apparatus.

Warm up activities
- Independent work – put together an individual sequence in which you try to prepare the body for vigorous activity by including movements that warm you up and stretch the body.
- Make your sequence map the initials of your name as you work.

Floor work
Whole body work
- Practise travelling on parts of the body following a pathway that is: curved; circular; square; zigzag. Can you make up your own pathway to follow?

Lower body work
- Travel on the feet to show quick, sudden changes in direction.
- Travel on the feet to show a wave-like air pattern with the body (jumps, leaps, skips etc.).
- Travel turning the body, using one leg to swing outwards to assist the body to turn. Follow a circular pathway. Try again following a different pathway.
- Focus on jumping skills showing varied air patterns.

Upper body work
- Take weight on hands and feet and complete a circle by moving the feet around the hands. Can you make a bigger and a smaller circle with the same actions?
- Travel from feet to hands to feet again, making: a square pathway; a circular pathway; a change of direction by bringing the feet down in different ways, e.g apart, together, close to the hands, far away from the hands etc.

Apparatus work (portable, linked, fixed)
- Varied pathways can be suggested by the imaginative positioning of mats (at angles to other apparatus, for example), sloping benches and other portable apparatus. Children should be encouraged to adopt a variety of starting points in preparing to use the apparatus, and to approach and leave the apparatus in varied directions.
- Travel on the apparatus following varied pathways: straight lines; zig-zag; curved. Any other pathway patterns to follow?
- Travel over the apparatus to show a variety of air patterns (by using different shapes).
- Link up two different pieces of apparatus using different pathways as you travel.
- On apparatus (ropes, bar, beam, sloping bench, box etc.) show a repetitive air pattern, before coming to the floor, to show a clear pathway while travelling.
- Show a high curving air pattern on to apparatus and a similar air pattern off. Emphasise 'height' in the jump and shallow jumps to maintain control.

Cool down activity
- On the floor map a pathway of movements that takes you away from where you start and takes you back to where you began. Make the pattern last no more than 10 seconds.

Pathways

Theme 6: Symmetry and Asymmetry

Learning to bring sharper, more defined shape to movement

Children will have covered ideas of symmetry and asymmetry at other points of their schooling. Here the concepts extend to how the body can move symmetrically and asymmetrically. Although the body itself is two-sided (bilateral) and symmetrical, few people use both sides with equal dexterity, and the majority of actions undertaken in everyday life have an asymmetrical stress. Symmetrical body movements demand control, coordination and body awareness, e.g. children on the whole find it easier to roll backwards over one shoulder than to roll straight when first learning the skill. A focus on this theme can help to develop the necessary control and this clearly also contributes to asymmetrical movement, which is more natural and therefore less limiting. Giving children the idea that their bodies can be divided vertically down the centre by an imaginary line helps them to develop an understanding that the body is said to be symmetrical if one side exactly mirrors the other. If opposite sides of the body are not moving at the same time and in the same way, or if one limb does not exactly mirror the corresponding limb, then the body is at that time asymmetrical. A strong focus for the discipline required of formal gymnastics comes from an attempt to perform agilities and to work on apparatus symmetrically. Very great control and precision are demanded by this work. There is a far greater variety of movements possible when working asymmetrically. By exploring both types of movement and contrasting them in sequences, the range of work is further developed and at a level conducive to the majority of children in this age band.

Warm up activities
- Individual limbering up, with a focus on long and held stretches and bending exercises.
- Practise balancing-on-hands skills.

Floor work
Whole body work
- Practise balancing the body on varied parts in which: one side of the body exactly mirrors the other; each side of the body and opposite limbs do not match.
- Practise rocking the body with both sides matching and then move into a symmetrical roll.
- Travel in different ways so that the two sides of the body are not balanced.
- Travel over the floor combining symmetrical and asymmetrical movements, sequence so that one type is followed by the other. How much variety can you achieve doing this?

Lower body work
- Practise jumping to show a symmetrical shape in the air (two feet to two feet).
- Jump to show irregular shapes in the air, e.g. twists, turns, one arm up, legs moving in different ways, etc.
- Perform a symmetrical jump and follow it immediately with an asymmetrical jump.
- Combine the above tasks with a variety of contrasting landings – symmetrical and asymmetrical.

Upper body work
- Travel in a variety of ways using the hands and feet to support the weight: symmetrically; asymmetrically.
- Take weight on the hands making the position of the legs at take off, the position of the legs in the air, the position of the legs on landing first symmetrical then asymmetrical.

Combined movements
- Put together a sequence that involves jumping, taking weight on hands and balancing, which: is symmetrical throughout; is asymmetrical throughout; contrasts the two.

Apparatus work (portable, linked, fixed)
- Find a variety of ways of supporting the body on the apparatus: symmetrically; asymmetrically.
- Travel using hands and feet: symmetrically; asymmetrically – move between the two alternately.
- Travel on any parts of the body using: symmetrical actions; asymmetrical actions.
- Create a sequence of symmetrical movements but show a jump or flight action in which the body is asymmetrical.
- Create a sequence of asymmetrical movements, but include one movement or balance where the body is symmetrical.

Cool down activity
- Repeat the performing of a symmetrical jump and follow it immediately with an asymmetrical jump. Work particularly on control and flow within this.

Symmetry and asymmetry

Theme 7: Balance and Continuity

Learning to achieve greater 'stillness' and its importance in linking to
other actions

Balance is the ability to hold the body still over a comparatively small
supporting base and is an area that will have been a feature of much previous
work. The theme is refocused here to further the understanding of the
concept of balance and to increase skill levels through further appreciation
of the techniques required to maintain a held position.

The continuity aspect is to develop these balancing skills within increasingly complex linked action and movement. In essence continuity involves
joining a series of movements together in such a way that one arises as a
natural outcome of the previous action, implying phrasing and timing.

Balance on small surfaces and points of the body requires control but there
is a danger that if balance is explored as a theme on its own the lesson can
become very static and one-paced. Stillness is an aspect of movement, and
stillness in a balanced position is best thought of as a position to be gained
following and preceding movement. In turn, the balance achieved is lost (but
not the control) as the body moves again.

Children will learn from this work that the greater the area supporting the
body (the base of support) and the more widely distributed the parts of
support, the easier it is to balance. Balance requires a certain body tension
if it is to be maintained on small and varied bases without unwanted movement – the achievement of 'stillness' in body action.

Warm up activities
- Practise a series of movements in which the body is wide and stretched.
- Practise twisting the body while taking weight on hands and feet – land
  back on feet every time.
- Show a series of balances on large, small and combinations of different
  support points (four-point balances, three-point balances, two, one etc.).

Floor work
Whole body work
- Find parts of the body on which you can balance. Practise stretching
  away from the floor.
- From standing, lower to balance on: shoulders; seat; chest. How can the
  use of the hands assist? Can you repeat without use of the hands?

Lower body work
- Practise balancing on one leg, varying the shape of the rest of the body
  (keep the other leg extended and tense).
- Find ways of balancing on different parts of the legs and feet: knees,
  heels, toes, sides of feet.

Upper body work
- Work on balancing for as long as possible with the weight on the hands.
  Are there different ways of doing this?

Balance and continuity

Combined movements
- Practise balancing on: four points of the body; three points; two points; one point. (Work on extending the body away from the floor.)
- Balance on four points when they are: far apart; close together. (Repeat, with three points and two points.)
- Select your favourite balances and find different ways of moving into and out of them. (Work on holding the balance achieved for a count of three seconds.)
- Plan a sequence of three balances in which the linking movements are smooth and controlled and lead naturally into one another.

Apparatus work (portable, linked, fixed)
- Travel on the apparatus but pause to hold one position of balance on hands and feet (for a count of three seconds).
- Move from the apparatus to the floor and try to balance on your hands using the apparatus as a support (hold this part of the action for three seconds), before completing the series of actions.
- Find places where you can balance on one part of the body – some large, some small, some combinations.
- Experiment with varied ways of moving into a balanced position while on the apparatus.

- Achieve a balance point on the apparatus, hold for a count of three, then slowly come out of that balance into another movement that allows movement to continue.
- Put together a sequence in which movement and balance blend smoothly one into the other. Try to make the sequence a set number of actions or spread over a time span (say 10 seconds).

Cool down activity
- Experiment further with practising wide and narrow bases of support in open space.

Theme 8: Flow

Learning to punctuate movement

As a natural follow-on to the previous theme here is another emphasising further qualitative elements of gymnastics work. If a sequence is to contain a number of contrasting elements then punctuation (moments when movement is slow or quick, or is paused) adds significantly to the work eventually produced. This theme explores the two contrasting aspects of flow, where action can actually be stopped, and the opposite in which the emphasis is on continuity of movement. Using both will bring greater interest and variety, and therefore extra quality to movement sequences.

Warm up activities
- Travel in free space on a variety of body parts at a slow pace and with control. Contrast by finishing with a quick movement.
- Create your own warm up sequence that concentrates on transferring body weight across all parts of the body.

Floor work
Whole body work
- Practise rocking on part of the body and then stop the movement, remaining in a steady, still position.
- Practise rolling and hold the body still in: a wide balance; a long narrow balance.
- Travel on parts of the body, emphasising continuity of movement. Try to keep the action flowing smoothly, avoiding pauses and jerky movements.
- Practise rolling forwards or backwards and add: a jump; a movement on the hands. (Remember to emphasise the need to link the movements smoothly.)

Lower body work
- Jump for height and hold a still position as soon as possible on landing. (Achieve a deep light landing, but try not to move the feet. Bend the knees on landing to assist this.)
- Jump for distance and hold a still position on landing. Repeat emphasis as above (gauge the depth of the landing to achieve this).
- Join running, jumps and changes of direction so that there are no pauses or breaks in the sequence, maintaining control and flow throughout.

Upper body work
- Practise taking weight on the hands in different ways and holding the balances achieved for at least three seconds. Do not start the count until 'stillness' is achieved.
- Find a number of varied ways (at least three) of moving from an upright position straight on to the hands.
- Experiment with varied ways of moving out of a position starting with weight on the hands, e.g. twist out, roll out, move to another balance.

Combined movements
- Practise moving continuously taking weight on the hands, then back to feet, and back again and so on.
- Create a floor sequence that includes four different movements that flow smoothly and include positions that are held (e.g. from start position into a jump, to a balance, to a roll, to a weight on hands movement, to finish).

Apparatus work (portable, linked, fixed)
- Find ways of getting on to the apparatus with: a jump; a roll; taking weight on hands, so that a position of stillness can be held as part of that sequence of action.
- Travel on the apparatus, and then stop the movement to show a definite body shape in a still position.
- Keep moving continuously from floor to apparatus, on the apparatus and back to the floor again, to show movements flowing easily together.
- Create a sequence on the apparatus that has two parts: one showing movement continuously checked in still positions; one where movements flow on without a pause. Alternate so that the first part is flow emphasised, and the second is checked.
- Plan and perform a sequence in which the actions show an interesting contrast between held positions and continuous, fluent movement.

Cool down activity
- Watch your partner contrast a series of movements and actions that feature pauses and flow. Comment on performance and offer suggestions for changing the routine.

Theme 9: Strength and Lightness

Learning to adjust muscular tension in movement

Children need to learn how to use their energy efficiently and economically. They have bodies that require activities that promote natural growth, for both fine and gross muscular development. The degree of strength employed needs to be appropriate to the different types of movement and actions performed. Many gymnastic activities require a degree of strong muscular tension, as in maintaining a balance that entails supporting body weight on small parts of the body, or in gripping and pulling on a rope or a beam to raise the body, or in taking off for a jump. It is very rare that the body is completely relaxed, for this would quite naturally result in a loss of control, but some movements require light muscular tension, particularly when the body is moving through the air or when rolling. Too much muscular tension can be fatiguing and too little can mean that movements lack control. Varied and more interesting gymnastic work will show varying degrees of strength and lightness. Strong, dynamic movements, particularly when associated with variations of speed and sudden changes of direction, should be used to show exciting highlights: for example, at the beginning of a sequence, during the series of movements being performed or to bring the sequence to a marked climax.

Warm up activities
- Create your own warm up sequence with two sections: strong, dynamic jumps and light landings; slow, controlled stretching movements on different parts of the body.

Floor work
Whole body work
- Lie face down on the floor and tense all the muscles, particularly the abdominal muscles (hold for a count of five). Release the tension and completely relax. Repeat.
- Roll gently, softly and lightly on the floor with little muscular tension.
- Practise holding a balance with strong muscular tension. Let the tension go slowly and bring a new part to the floor for another strong balance.

Lower body work
- Jump upwards with a vigorous thrust with the legs (from a deep, springy starting position). Lift the chest and relax for a light landing, but tense the body again to show a controlled and balanced finish.
- Travel on the feet to show the following contrasts: slowly and lightly; quickly and lightly; slowly and strongly; quickly and strongly.

Upper body work
- Place the hands on the floor lightly, take your weight on your hands and bring your feet back to the floor with a minimum of muscular tension. Make a light landing (listen to it).
- Practise trying to hold the weight on the hands with sufficient tension to achieve stillness.

Combined movements
- Take up a position on the floor with your front or back in contact with the surface and move the body slowly across the space using body strength to pull, push and twist.
- Travel over the floor showing a contrast between slow, strong movements and quick, light movements.

Apparatus work (portable, linked, fixed)
- Find a variety of places on the apparatus where you can move using a great deal of strength, e.g. pushing, pressing, heaving and pulling.
- Find different ways of moving on the apparatus so that little energy needs to be expended, e.g. sliding, jumping down, swinging, rolling and circling.
- Starting on the floor travel slowly and with lightness and build up to a quick, strong movement – take this onto apparatus.
- Reverse the above – begin with a strong, vigorous movement and finish with a slow, light movement.
- Contrast curling and stretching movements on the apparatus in which the curled movements are relaxed and the stretched movements are done with strong muscular tension. Reverse the emphasis.
- Create a sequence on the apparatus that has a clearly defined highlight and a climax at the end. Include strong and lighter elements in the series of actions.

Cool down activity
- Perform two contrasting linked movements that show strength and lightness in execution. Show to your partner and invite comment.

Strength and lightness

11 Further Gymnastic Themes

Themes Emphasising the 'Body' Aspects of Movement

Locomotion

This is an elementary theme that is worthy of inclusion in the early years work, because it is primarily concerned with travelling and stopping skills. Such a concentrated focus will support children's exploration of different ways of moving from A to B, and serve the need to gain steadily, over time, improved bodily control in the workspaces provided.

Balance

This theme is worth visiting in isolation, again early in children's exploration and experimentation stage, and when concentrating on finding out what their bodies are capable of. Balance is the ability to hold the body over a range of large and small supporting bases, and teaches children about large and small body parts. The overall aims of the theme are to provide an understanding of the concept (and 'feeling') of balance and to increase levels of skill through an appreciation of the different techniques required to maintain a 'held' position for short and longer periods.

Simple linking

As a precursor for 'Joining Movements' (and later 'Sequences') this theme develops the ability to join movements together so that they follow one another increasingly smoothly. The theme in essence establishes the concept of linked movements compared with two individual movements performed in succession, and aims to extend skill through concentration on the need to finish one movement balanced and in a position to follow on into a second. Clearly this is the beginning of work that will eventually result in successful sequence work much later down the line, and should be concentrated within the early work covered in gymnastic units of work.

Body awareness

Here is a theme that can add polish and enhanced quality to finished sequence work, on floor and apparatus. Its focus lies in an awareness of how any part of the body is moving and the effect that this has on the body as a whole. Ultimately, awareness should be through the 'feel' of a movement, without a need to rely on visual or intellectual cues. Although this is a fundamental characteristic of all movement, the theme can be very useful in improving quality of performance through its emphasis on the need for awareness of all body parts in order to achieve a stylish, complete and finished performance.

Themes Emphasising the 'Dynamic' Aspects of Movement

Acceleration and deceleration

This theme is clearly related to that of 'Speed', but with a stronger focus on more gradual changes of speed. This is also a useful area of work to engage in for improving overall control of movement and increasing the variety and aesthetic qualities to be aimed for in sequence work.

Rhythm and timing

When children are working as individuals, work in this particular area imparts a growing awareness of the timing of preparation, action and recovery, and consequently the rhythmic pattern that assists efficient performance of particular skills. At a more advanced level, the theme also involves using accent, timing, phrasing and repetition in order to compose movement sequences in pairs, threes or larger groups. In addition to developing further a sense of phrasing and timing when composing sequences, the theme encourages members of such groups to conform to various set rhythmic patterns and to experiment with the effect of altering these in a given movement phrase.

Themes Emphasising the 'Relationships' Aspects of Movement

Relation to floor and apparatus

An elementary theme, this may be useful in ensuring that all the possibilities of a situation are explored. For example, in relation to the floor the body may be facing, away from, sideways to, the right way up or upside down. With apparatus there are huge possibilities of going under, over, around, along, across, up, down, on, off etc.

Partner work

Under this general theme almost any work covered can be developed by combining work with a partner in some way. There are various aspects of this theme that can be explored in their own right.

Matching actions

This is when a pair look to perform as exactly as possible the same actions, at the same time or one after the other. Further possibilities come from a choice of starting position, e.g. side by side facing the same position, side by side facing different directions, facing each other and mirroring the other's movements, back to back, one behind the other facing in the same direction. Some of the work here presents a greater challenge because the partner will be out of sight for shorter or longer periods during the performance of the matched actions. This theme can therefore extend skill by adapting movement to match that of a partner. This may involve using, for example, a different foot for take-off, or performing a movement such as a cartwheel in the opposite direction from that preferred by the individual child.

Making and negotiating obstacles (without contact)

This work will involve adapting to a partner's movement and actions so that one goes over or round the other, or through potential 'holes' formed by one for the other to negotiate. The theme requires a sound understanding of weight bearing and balance, together with an ability to assess the partner's skill when making the obstacles so that impossible tasks are not set. The composition of a sequence where both partners take both sides requires inventiveness and creativity of thinking in planning, skill in performance and good timing for smooth execution.

Partner work (with contact)

This work requires greater dependence on one another, and therefore an enhanced sense of responsibility. A can help B to maintain a balance to achieve flight: for example, A can provide a base of support for B to balance on or push off from to achieve flight. True interdependence can be achieved through work on counterbalance and countertension. Counterbalance involves leaning or pushing against each other with the weight adjusted in such a way that neither could retain the position without the help of the other. The supporting bases of the partners will be wide apart. Countertension is a position of similar interdependence achieved with bases close together and the partners pulling against one another.

Lifting, carrying and lowering

This is an advanced theme, related to and demanding body control, strength and skill. It is probably better suited, in the primary school setting, to work in threes rather than twos. Similar counterbalance and countertension possibilities exist here as in the theme above, but with greater potential for collaborative work to be more complex with the addition of an extra person involved. (This could also be a theme visited very much earlier in the programme of children's gymnastics work, when teaching the basics of lifting, carrying and manoeuvring apparatus, particularly in terms of the cooperative nature of such activities.)

Work in Threes

All aspects of partner work can also be used for work in threes. This extends the possibilities, particularly in work with contact, so that two individuals control the balance, flight and placing of a third. The theme particularly encourages cooperation in the group situation, and extends movement vocabulary and experience, especially in situations where two can help a third to perform a movement that they might otherwise be incapable of performing if left to their own efforts alone.

Partner work

Appendix 1
Record Sheets for
Assessment of Pupil Progress

Key Stage 1 Gymnastics

By the end of the key stage pupils should be able to:

Pupil's name	Plan • Joining together linked movements and actions, e.g. jumps, rolls and balances.	Comments
	Perform • *Skills*: perform basic gymnastic actions with increasing control and precision, showing a change of direction, shape or speed. • *Skills*: perform chosen specific skills from the basic actions of jumping, rolling, balancing, travelling on hands and feet; and in climbing, hanging and swinging.	
	Evaluate • Recognise own and others' individual actions and skills and within joined movement sequences.	
	Health • Recognise the importance of warming up before exercise and warming down as a conclusion to activity. • Recognise that exercise causes the heart to beat faster, that there is a knock-on effect to body temperature, that breathing can get faster and that the body can get tired.	
	Safety • Lift, carry, site, assemble and dismantle apparatus with teacher supervision. • Safely share the workspace provided, including when working on apparatus.	
	PSHE • Collaborate and cooperate with others in gymnastics work. • Comment constructively on own and others' work.	

Pupils' progress can be coded by: 1, working towards; 2, achieved; 3, achievement 'plus'.

Key Stage 2 Gymnastics

By the end of the key stage pupils should be able to:

Pupil's name	Plan	Comments
	• Extended sequences of at least five or six movements joined together and including changes of speed, shape and direction and performance at different levels on floor and apparatus.	
	Perform • *Skills*: perform selected gymnastic skills that increasingly show clear body shape, extension, accuracy and control. • *Skills*: sequence selected actions that are linked together with increasing control, flow and continuity. • *Skills*: extended, repeatable and more complex sequences that have defined start and finish positions. • *Skills*: perform gymnastic actions that match the context, e.g. floor to apparatus, individual, pairs or groupwork.	
	Evaluate • Using given criteria, provide accurate and insightful feedback to self and others. • Identify accurately the component parts and features of a sequence. • Comment on the quality of actions in relation to speed, direction and body shape achieved.	
	Health • Display increasing knowledge of which particular activities are suitable for gymnastics warming up. • Understand the need to combine pulse-raising activity and stretching exercises for warm up and warm down parts of each lesson.	
	Safety • Safely apply lifting, carrying, siting, assembly and dismantling of apparatus skills. • Safely share the workspace and the apparatus with due concern for own and others' safety.	
	PSHE • Work collaboratively and cooperatively with others. • Display understanding of and sensitivity to others' abilities.	

Pupils' progress can be coded by: 1, working towards; 2, achieved; 3, achievement 'plus'.

Appendix 2 The Content of Primary Gymnastic Activity: Movement Vocabulary

Themes of Key Stages 1 and 2

- Space
- Use of apparatus
- Movement tasks
- Supporting body weight
- Transference of weight
- Lifting parts high
- Travelling
- Feet together and apart
- Curling and stretching
- Use of Space
- Transferring weight
- Joining movements
- Directions
- Parts together and apart
- Lifting and lowering
- Shape
- Speed
- Twisting and turning
- Sequences
- Levels
- Partner work
- Flight
- Pathways
- Symmetry and asymmetry
- Balance and continuity
- Flow
- Strength and lightness

Skills

Stability
- Balance
- Stillness
- Dynamic
- Inverted
- On different body parts

Locomotion
- Walking
- Jogging
- Skipping
- Galloping
- Running
- Jumping
- Rolling
- On different body parts
- Continuous
- Paused

Manipulative
- Grasp
- Grip
- Hook
- Hang
- Spring
- Push
- Pull
- Slide

Body

Whole body
- Large parts
- Small parts
- Fixed
- Free
- Near
- Far
- Leading
- Following
- Isolated

Surface
- Front
- Back
- Side
- Top
- Bottom
- On different body parts

Shape
- Arrow
- Ball
- Wall
- Twist
- Gesture

Size
- Big
- Small
- Medium

Spatial

Personal
- Near
- Next to
- Far away
- In front
- Behind
- At the side
- Following
- Leading

General
- Directions
- Forwards
- Backwards
- Sideways
- Diagonal
- Up/down

Levels
- High
- Low
- Medium
- Near floor
- Away from the floor

Pathways
- Straight
- Circular
- Square
- Curved
- Rectangular
- Angular
- Zigzag
- Indirect

Dynamics

Speed
- Go and stop
- Fast
- Slow
- Quicker
- Accelerate
- Decelerate
- Slower
- Short time
- Long time
- Sudden
- Stillness

Weight
- Strong
- Powerful
- Firm
- Light
- Soft
- Tension

Time
- At same time
- Within a set time
- After another
- Before another
- Use same space

Apparatus

Portable
- Mini-apparatus
- Hoops
- Cones
- Skipping ropes
- Bean bags
- Skittles
- Canes
- Discs
- Mats
- Benches
- Linking planks
- Nesting tables
- A frames
- Ladders
- Movement tables
- Boxes
- Stools

Fixed
- Frames
- Ropes
- Beams
- Bars
- Poles

Relationships

Individual

Partner

Groups

Class
- Work alone
- Work with others
- Copy
- Contrast
- Mirror/match
- Support actions
- Talk and discuss movement

Movement skill vocabulary

- On to
- Off
- Across
- Between
- Up
- Down
- Over
- Under
- Around
- Next to
- Far away from
- Through
- Underneath
- Into
- Out of
- Near to
- Towards
- Away from
- Height
- Length
- Width
- Obstacle

Resources

Bibliography

BAALPE (1999) *Safe Practice in Physical Education*. Dudley: British Association of Advisers and Lecturers in Physical Education.

Benn, T. and Benn, B. (1992) *Primary Gymnastics: A Multi Activities Approach*. Cambridge: Cambridge University Press.

Buckland, D. (1969) *Gymnastics: Activity in the Primary School*. London: Heinemann.

Carroll, M. E. and Manners, H. K. (1991) *Gymnastics 7–11: A Session by Session Approach to Key Stage 2*. London: Falmer Press.

DfEE (1999) *Physical Education in the National Curriculum*. London: DfEE and QCA.

DfEE (2000) *Curriculum Guidance for the Foundation Stage*. London: DfEE.

DfEE and QCA (2000) *A Scheme of Work for Key Stages 1 and 2: Physical Education*. London: DfEE and QCA.

Davies, A. and Sabin, V. (1995) *Body Work: Primary Children: Dance and Gymnastics*. Cheltenham: Stanley Thornes.

Hall, J. (1995) *Gymnastic Activities for Juniors*. London: A & C Black.

Hall, J. (1996) *Gymnastic Activities for Infants*. London: A & C Black.

Jackman, J. and Currier, B. (1992) *Gymnastic Skills and Games*. London: A & C Black.

Manners, H. K. and Carroll, M. E. (1991) *Gymnastics 4–7: A Session by Session Approach to Key Stage 1*. London: Falmer Press.

Manners, H. K. and Carroll, M. E. (1995) *A Framework for Physical Education in the Early Years*. London: Falmer Press.

Martin, B., McCarthy, A. and Lukins, C. (1994) *Dice and Spinners: New Ideas for Teaching Gymnastics*. Nottingham: Davies Sports.

Maude, T. (1997) *Gymnastics*. London: Hodder & Stoughton.

Pain, S., Price, L., Forest-Jones, G. and Longhurst, J. (1997) *Find a Space! A Primary Teacher's Guide to Physical Education and Health-related Exercise*. London: David Fulton Publishers.

Penny, S., Ford, R., Price, L. and Young, S. (2002) *Teaching Arts in Primary Schools*. Exeter: Learning Matters.

Stewart, D. (1990) *The Right to Movement: Motor Development in Every School*. London: Falmer Press.

Wetton, P. (1997) *Physical Education in the Early Years*. London: Routledge.

Other resources of practical use

BAGA Award Schemes. Teaching materials.

Task Cards for Gymnastics. Primrose Publishing Ltd.

Dance, Games and Gymnastics for the Primary School. Lessons for your PE programme: Primrose Publishing Ltd.

Gymnastics. In the *Know the Game* series. A & C Black.

Persil 'Funfit'. National Curriculum resource pack for Key Stages 1 and 2 PE.

LEA teaching materials for gymnastics (specifically Clywd, Coventry, Devon, Dudley, Harrow, Hertfordshire, Leeds, Sutton and West Sussex LEAs).

Video materials, e.g. *Expectations in Physical Education at Key Stage 1 and 2*, (SCAA) and *The Gym Kit* (Homerton College, Cambridge).

Journals

British Journal of Teaching Physical Education
Bulletin of Physical Education
PE and Sport
Sports Teacher

Websites

www.baalpe.org: British Association of Advisers and Lecturers in Physical Education
www.british-gymnastics.org: British Gymnastics Association
www.ccpr.org.uk: Central Council for Physical Recreation
www.english.sports.gov.uk: English Sports
www.pe.central.vt.edu: PE Central
www.pelinks4u.org: PE Links
www.peprimary.co.uk: PE Primary
www.teleschool.org.uk/PEA: Physical Education Association UK
www.sportengland.org: Sport England
www.sportscotland.org.uk: Sport Scotland
www.uksport.gov.uk: UK Sport
www.youthsport.net: Youth Sport Trust

Equipment

To ensure that effective delivery of the statutory requirement for gymnastic activity can take place the following apparatus is necessary. These lists should also assist schools when considering their own particular needs and looking to purchase or procure further apparatus.

Fixed apparatus (wall hinged)

- Climbing frame(s) to include linking bar(s), beam(s), ladder(s), rope/swinging attachments, etc.

Portable apparatus (including linking equipment)

- Sets of nesting/activity tables.
- Movement table.
- Benches (wooden/padded).
- Wooden agility planks.
- Mats (enough for at least one between two) of a size and weight to suit the whole age range.
- Trestles (A frames, etc.).
- Stools.
- Boxes – section and bar.
- Balance beam(s).
- Springboard(s).

Additionally, it is always useful to use 'other' traditional PE equipment, such as skipping ropes, cones, skittles, bean bags and hoops, to present alternative challenges and tasks using familiar equipment used in other activities. They lend colour and different shapes, and can combine to make different types of structures around which children can move. They can also serve the very useful and practical purpose of adding to what might be a limited provision of 'typical' gymnastic equipment.

Index

Note: 'p' after a page number indicates a photograph, or photograph and text.

acceleration, as theme 102
apparatus 16, 21, 110–11
  asymmetry, symmetry and 91
  balance and 94–5p
  curling, stretching and 45
  directions and 60
  feet and 27, 42–3
  flight and 83–4, 86
  flow and 97
  hands and 27, 42
  joining movement and 57
  levels in space and 78–9
  lifting, lowering body and 41, 63–4
  lightness, strength and 99
  natural movement and 29, 30
  parts of body and 61
  pathways and 89
  relation to, as theme 102
  scope 24–5, 27–8, 38
  sequences of movement and 75, 76
  shape and 66
  space and 24, 47, 48
  speed and 69–70
  supporting body weight and 33, 34p
  as theme 24–8p
  transferring body weight and 36, 52–3, 54
  travelling and 38, 40
  turning, twisting and 71
assessment 105–6
  flight and 87
  natural movement and 31
  scope 15–17
  sequences of movement and 77
  space and 48, 49
  transferring weight and 54, 55
  travelling and 38–9
asymmetry, symmetry and, as theme 90–2p
attainment 105–6
  flight and 87
  individual 2, 3, 4, 5, 6, 12, 13–14, 16–17, 18
  natural movement and 31
  realism in 8, 12, 15
  scope 10–11
  sequences of movement and 77

  space and 49
  transferable skills from 11–12
  transferring weight and 55
  travelling and 39

balance
  asymmetry, symmetry and 90
  natural movement and 30
  as theme 93–5p, 101
  transferring body weight and 54
benches 27
benchmarks 10, 12
body 1, 3, 6
  control in 17
  in themes *see individual terms*
  weight 33–6p, 51–5p
  see also lower body; upper body; whole body
body awareness, as theme 101–2

canes 25
carrying, lifting, lowering and, as theme 103–4
changing clothes 15
climbing 70p
  apparatus and 26
clothes 21
  changing 15
club, gym 19–20
collaboration 17
  see also groups; partners
cones 25
confidence 6, 7, 10, 16
consolidation 2, 4, 6, 8
  see also individual terms
contrasting, by partners 80
control
  asymmetry, symmetry and 90–2p
  of body 17
  sequences of movement and 74p
creativity, scope 16
curling, stretching and, as theme 44–5p

deceleration, as theme 102
demonstration 15
directions, as theme 59–60p

energy 6
evaluation 105, 106
    from observation 17–18
experience, prior 7
extracurricular work 19–20

feet
    apparatus and 27
    bare foot work 21
    curling, stretching and 44
    flight and 83
    hands and 42, 88–9p
    lifting, lowering body and 63
    natural movement and 28, 29
    parts of body and 61
    pathways and 88–9p
    space and 24
    as theme 42–3p
    transferring body weight and 35–6
first lessons 14–15
first tasks 15
    see also individual terms
flight, as theme 83–7p
floor
    relation to, as theme 102
    work on *see individual terms*
flow 17
    as theme 96–7p
    see also sequences of movement
following, by partners 80
fours, groups of 82
frameworks 1, 2
    on flight 86–7
    on natural movement 30–1
    on sequences of movement 76–7
    on space 48–9
    on transferring body weight 54–5
    on travelling 38–9

games 6
goals
    flight and 87
    natural movement and 31
    sequences of movement and 77
    space and 49
    transferring weight and 55
    travelling and 39
groups 16
    carrying, lifting, lowering and 103–4
    flight and 86
    of four 82
    natural movement and 30
    from partners 82
    sequences of movement and 76–7
    space and 48
    of three 82, 104
    travelling and 38–9
    see also collaboration
gym club 19–20

hands
    apparatus and 27
    feet and 42, 88–9p
    flight and 83
    flow and 96–7
    lifting, lowering body and 63
    natural movement and 29
    parts of body and 61
    pathways and 88–9p
    space and 24
    transferring body weight and 36
handstanding 52
hanging 26p, 32p, 50p
health and safety 16, 21–2, 105, 106
hoops 25

inclusion 10
individual attainment 2, 3, 4, 12, 16–17, 18
    balanced aims for 13–14
    motor development and 5, 6
individuals *see individual terms*
intervention 13

joining movement, as theme 56–7
jumping 32p, 58p
    asymmetry, symmetry and 90–1
    feet and 42
    flight and 83–4, 86
    joining movement and 56–7
    natural movement and 29, 30

key skills 17
    locomotion as 101
knowledge 16, 19

landing 62p
    flight and 83–4, 86
    natural movement and 28, 29
language, terminology 2, 7
    in context 19
    scope 8, 107
legs
    balance and 93
    feet and 42
    shape and 66
levels in space, as theme 78–9
life skills 4, 16
    observation as 8, 9, 17–18
    problem-solving as 6
lifting
    carrying, lowering and, as theme 103–4
    lowering body and, as theme 63–4p
    parts of body, as theme 40–1p
lightness, strength and, as theme 98–100p
linking movement 17
    joining movement from 56–7
    sequences of movement from 8–9, 73–7p, 79–
        83p, 93–7p
    as theme 101

locomotion, as theme 101
lower body 7
  apparatus and 27
  asymmetry, symmetry and 90–1
  balance and 93
  bare foot work 21
  curling, stretching and 44
  flight and 83
  flow and 96
  joining movement and 56
  levels in space and 78
  lightness, strength and 98
  natural movement and 28
  parts of body and 61
  pathways and 88–9p
  sequences of movement and 74
  space and 24, 47, 48
  speed and 69
  supporting body weight and 33
  as theme 42–3
  transferring body weight and 35, 36, 51
  travelling and 37
  turning, twisting and 71
lowering
  carrying, lifting and, as theme 103–4
  lifting body and, as theme 63–4p

matching
  asymmetry, symmetry and 90–2p
  by partners 80
  as theme 103
mats 27
motor development 3–4
  asymmetry and symmetry as 90–2p
  balance as 30, 54, 90, 93–5p, 101
  basic movement as 7
  directions as 59–60p
  individual attainment and 5, 6
  muscle development as 98–100p
  rhythm as 102
  scope 5
  space as *see* space
  speed as 69–70, 96, 97, 102
movement *see individual terms*
muscle development, lightness, strength and
    98–100p
music, sequences of movement and 76–7

National Curriculum 10–12
  scope 5
natural movement 1
  scope 28
  as theme 28–31

observation 8, 9
  evaluation from 17–18
obstacles, partners as 81
  as theme 103

partners 8, 9
  flight and 86
  individuals and 79
  natural movement and 30
  sequences of movement and 76–7
  space and 48
  as theme 79–83p, 102, 103
  transferring weight and 54
  travelling and 38–9
  see also collaboration
parts of body
  lifting, as theme 40–1p
  as theme 61
passing, by partners 81
pathways, as theme, scope 88–9p
PE 6
  scope 5
  transferable skills in 3, 4
planning
  for partner work 79–80
  by records 18–19, 105–6
  for secondary school 20
play 6, 7
problem-solving 6

quality of work 17

rationale 3–4
realism in attainment 8, 12, 15
record sheet, attainment in 105–6
record-keeping 18–19
resources 2, 49
  apparatus *see* apparatus
  multimedia 109, 110
  texts 109, 110
rhythm, as theme 102
rolling, natural movement and 30
running, space and 23

safety 16, 21–2, 105, 106
secondary school 20
self-esteem 6, 7, 10, 16
sequences of movement 8–9
  balance and 93–5p
  flow and 96–7p
  partners and 79–83p
  as theme 73–7p
  see also flow
shape
  curling, stretching and 44–5p
  as theme 65–8p
skittles 25
space 16
  flight and 83–7p
  levels in 78–9
  pathways and 88–9
  relation in *see individual terms*
  as theme 23–4, 46–9

3 1854 007 693 800

speed
   flow and 96, 97
   as theme 69–70, 102
sport 6
stillness
   balance and 93
   flow and 96, 97
strength, lightness and, as theme 98–100p
stretching, curling and, as theme 44–5p
supporting
   of body weight 33–4p
   by partners 81–2p
sustainability 16
symmetry, asymmetry and, as theme 90–2p

terminology 2, 7
   in context 19
   scope 8, 107
themes *see individual terms*
threes, groups of 82
   as theme 104
time
   with apparatus 24
   progress through 15–17
   in speed 69–70
timing
   sequences of movement and 76–7
   as theme 102
transferable skills 3, 4, 6, 11–12, 17, 19
   curling, stretching and 45
   directions and 60
   sequences of movement and 76
   transferring body weight and 36
   turning, twisting and 72
transferring body weight, as theme 34–6p,
      51–5p
travelling
   curling, stretching and 44
   feet and 42
   scope 38
   space and 46
   speed and 69–70
   as theme 36–40p
turning, twisting and, as theme 71–2

understanding 16, 19
unique challenges 1
upper body 7
   apparatus and 27

asymmetry, symmetry and 91
curling, stretching and 44
flight and 83
flow and 96
joining movement and 57
levels in space and 78
lifting, lowering body and 40, 63
lightness, strength and 98
natural movement and 29
parts of body and 61
pathways and 88–9p
shape and 66
space and 24, 47, 48
speed and 69
supporting body weight and 33
transferring body weight and 36, 52
travelling and 37, 42
turning, twisting and 71

vocabulary 2, 7
   in context 19
   scope 8, 107

websites 110
weight, body
   supporting 33–4p
   transferring 34–6p, 51–5p
whole body 16
   asymmetry, symmetry and 90
   balance and 93
   curling, stretching and 44
   directions and 59
   feet and 42
   flow and 96
   joining movement and 56
   levels in space and 78
   lifting, lowering body and 40, 63
   lightness, strength and 98
   natural movement and 28, 30
   parts of body and 61
   sequences of movement and 73
   shape and 65
   space and 23, 46, 48
   speed and 69
   supporting body weight and 33
   transferring body weight and 35p, 51
   travelling and 37, 38–9
   turning, twisting and 71
whole education *see* transferable skills